THE KOREAN CRISIS

One Nation, Two Peoples, A World On The Brink

JACK VAN DER SLIK

WILDBLUE PRESS

WildBluePress.com

THE KOREAN CRISIS published by:

WILDBLUE PRESS

P.O. Box 102440

Denver, Colorado 80250

ISBN 978-1-947290-17-4   Trade Paperback

ISBN 978-1-947290-16-7   eBook

Interior Formatting/Book Cover Design by Elijah Toten

www.totencreative.com

TABLE OF CONTENTS

PROLOGUE: PRESENT CIRCUMSTANCES IN THE DIVIDED KOREAN PENINSULA, 2016

The 38th parallel north is a map maker's latitudinal circle around the Earth. It crosses North America, the Atlantic Ocean, and Europe, including the Mediterranean Sea, Asia, and the Pacific Ocean. But nowhere does it have greater political significance than on the Korean Peninsula. There it cuts that countryside into approximately equal sized halves. Americans know those two parts as South Korea and North Korea; or, more politically correct, as the Republic of Korea (ROK) and the Democratic People's Republic of Korea (DPRK). That boundary line, created after World War II by agreement between the United States and the Soviet Union, was hugely contested in 1950-1953 by the Korean War. That conflict was settled only with a ceasefire armistice, and to this day, that line, euphemistically called the DMZ (demilitarized zone), remains the most militaristically reinforced boundary in the world. There are barricades, barbed wire, thousands of guard posts, bunkers for troops, heavy weapons emplacements, rocket launchers, armed soldiers, and millions of land mines on both sides of the line to keep the two nations apart.

In North Korea, the prominent, single person atop an elite that governs about twenty-four million North Koreans is an impetuous young leader, born on January 8, 1984: Kim Jong Un. He was installed in his singular top position in 2011 upon the death of his father, Kim Jong Il, who in 1998 succeeded his father, Kim Il Sung, North Korea's "Great Leader" during and after the Korean War. The North Korean people continue to regard Kim Il Sung as the nation's "Eternal President." While outside observers initially thought the transition to Kim Jong Un was precarious, Kim has established himself as a vigorous and visible leader. In 2016, he boldly called for the first full meeting of the Korean Workers' Party (KWP) in thirty-six years. In preparation, he mobilized the country with what was called a seventy day workers loyalty campaign. During the four day party convention for three thousand KWP members in May 2016, Kim promoted a national agenda emphasizing a two-pronged policy of economic development and greater nuclear weapon capability. The KWP ceremoniously added to his titles by making him their party chairman (previously he was simply first secretary). After sending the party members home following a rapturous concluding ceremony, the regime announced a two hundred-day challenge called a loyalty campaign. Citizens everywhere were called upon to increase their work efforts to finish building projects, add to production in the factories and fields, and generally boost their support for the KWP in every feasible way. Another follow-up to the party convention was the announced reconvening of the Supreme People's Assembly, the DPRK's legislature, at the end of June. This Assembly would ratify policies to implement the directions established by the KWP convention decisions.

It is noteworthy to itemize some of the initiatives taken under Kim's vigorous leadership. Kim opened 2016 visibly with an elaborate New Year's Day speech. He called on his people to believe in the efficacy of the "*Juche* revolution." It asserts the priority of North Korea's self-development through a socialist economy. "Worship of big countries and dependence on foreign forces is the road to national ruin; self-development alone is the road to sustaining the dignity of our country ... With affection, trust, dignity and pride in everything of our own, we should achieve the great cause of building and realize the people's dreams and ideals without fail by our own efforts, technology and resources." The official line is that North Korea prospers best by its own self-contained system and society.

Kim did not ignore the international neighborhood. (Note in the following quote that the transcript does not capitalize the *S* when referring to its neighbor, *South* Korea.)

> Today the Peninsula has become the hottest spot in the world and a hotbed of war owing to the U. S. aggressive strategy for the domination of Asia and its reckless moves for a war against the DPRK. The U. S. And south Korea war maniacs are conducting large-scale military exercises aimed at nuclear war against the DPRK ... [They] must discontinue their extremely dangerous aggressive war exercises ... that aggravates tension in the Korean Peninsula ... However, if aggressors dare to provoke us, though to a slight degree, we will never tolerate it but respond resolutely with a merciless sacred war of justice, a great war for national reunification (Kim Jong Un, New Year Address, January 1, 2016).

Within a week of his New Year's Day address, Kim Jong Un boasted that his country successfully conducted its fourth nuclear bomb test – he went so far as to claim it was a hydrogen bomb. That claim was quickly discounted by Western analysts. An *Associated Press* report told of celebration with banners and confetti in Pyongyang when the news about the January 6 nuclear test success was announced. There were immediate activities at the United Nations to stiffen sanctions against North Korea. Park Gyun Hye, then the president of South Korea, took counsel with her national security aides. Japan condemned the test. Even China, North Korea's closest ally, said it was opposed to the North Korean nuclear explosion. But in his own country, Kim, who celebrated a birthday a couple of days later, was solidifying his hold on the reins of power in North Korea. "On Friday, North Korea released television coverage of footage, part of a documentary glorifying Mr. Kim's leadership" (Choe, *New York Times*, January 8, 2016).

In early February, the DPRK launched an Earth observation satellite into orbit, reportedly at the direct order of Kim Jong Un. The success was publicized to the North Korean people in a special television broadcast by Korean Central Television. According to the *Washington Post* report, North Korea said the launch was "for scientific purposes, but analysts and many governments see this as a disguised missile test. North Korea has successfully launched short- and medium-range missiles but has been working to develop a reliable long-range intercontinental ballistic missile, capable of reaching the West Coast of the United States" (Fifield, *Washington Post*, February 6, 2016).

In March, a DPRK news agency bragged about its hydrogen bomb, threatening that "if this H-bomb were to be mounted on an intercontinental ballistic missile and fall on Manhattan in New York City, all the people there would be killed immediately and the city would burn to ashes" (Fifield, *Washington Post*, March 13, 2016). While American military experts discounted the capability of North Korean intercontinental rocketry, the crass effrontery of North Korea's published threats are disturbing.

In the spring of 2016, there were more DPRK provocations. North Korea made repeated, but unsuccessful, attempts to launch intermediate-range missiles. The failures took place on April 15 and 29. In May, there was another failure with the Musudan missile fired from a mobile launcher (Schilling, June 1, 2016). On April 23, North Korea tested a submarine-launched ballistic missile. The US Strategic Command confirmed that it detected the launch, and South Korea reported that the missile flew only thirty kilometers. Nevertheless, this too adds to the threat capabilities of North Korea. It is true, of course, that failure with missiles is not uniquely a North Korean problem. The US has had its share of failures while engaged in the learning process associated with weapons development. However, when the DPRK rights its technology, Japan, South Korea, and the Philippines, along with American targets on Guam and Okinawa, are vulnerable to North Korean weapons. Commenting on the submarine missile launch, an American expert stated: "North Korea has an experimental testbed that reliably launched to a range of 30 km, maybe from a submarine or a submerged barge. We don't know. But it is increasingly clear a real, albeit limited, submarine missile threat from North Korea will probably emerge by the year 2020" (Schilling, April 25, 2016).

During the rest of 2016 and into 2017, North Korea has continued its missile testing. Its focus on missiles has produced successes in middle-range solid fueled rockets that are mobile and therefore more elusive. Able to be hidden in mountain caves, they could be rolled out and quickly launched. There were about a dozen firings in 2017, acts that defied United Nations' sanctions. Kim has announced his intent to increase the range of his weapons in order to strike the American mainland.

In May 2016, having brought together the 7th Congress of the Korean Workers' Party delegates, Kim Jong Un boasted about the nuclear explosion in January and the intercontinental rocket launch in February. He claimed that these UN forbidden feats confirmed the "dignity and national power of *Juche* Korea at the highest level." Kim's *juche* ideology justifies having a powerful, nuclear-armed North Korea to assure itself about its future survival in the face of hostile forces outside that country, specifically South Korea and the US (Choe, *New York Times*, May 6, 2016). To underscore his intentions, Kim ordered up another successful nuclear explosion in September, a weapon twice as powerful as the one set off in January. Its effectiveness was confirmed by reliable seismologists whose detection instruments could measure its effects. In 2017, American observers predicted a sixth nuclear test explosion still to come.

Although President Obama was largely silent regarding the North Korean provocations, the American military was quietly active. In March 2016, joint military exercises engaged 300,000 South Korean troops along with 17,000

American soldiers and Marines. Considering the aggressive threats and military activities in the DPRK, the South Korean Defense Ministry said that the year's exercises were the biggest ever. The US added visibility to the operations by bringing a nuclear powered aircraft carrier to the Korean waters. A couple of special efforts marked the exercises. There were joint actions, including simulations of "surgical strikes" to knock out the North Korean leadership in Pyongyang. Another exercise was a two-day medical evacuation drill for handling simulated casualties. The result? Greater military readiness for coordinated action by US and ROK troops in case of a military attack from the DPRK.

Not surprisingly, these joint operations evoked a noisy, threatening North Korean response: "The Revolutionary Armed Forces of the DPRK are fully ready to preempt merciless and annihilating strikes at the enemies if they show even the slightest sign of provocation" (Fifield, *Washington Post*, March 16, 2016).

In a spiteful tit-for-tat action, a University of Virginia student visiting North Korea in an organized tour during the New Year's holiday was imprisoned for attempting to steal a North Korean propaganda banner. Convicted of "hostile acts against the state" of North Korea, Otto Wambier was sentenced to fifteen years in prison with hard labor. What would to Americans look like a dormitory prank by a visiting student was treated by the DPRK Supreme Court as a severely punishable crime. Perhaps Wambier's real mistake was in being in North Korea at the time the US and South Korea were conducting their annual military drills. (See Fifield, *Washington Post*, March 18, 2016.) Wambier was held prisoner for more than a year. A seriously disabled Wambier was released and sent home to his parents in June 2017. North Koreans said he contracted botulism and became comatose. At home in Cincinnati, doctors diagnosed Wambier with brain damage caused by a heart attack that cut off blood flow to his brain; he remained in a state of "unresponsive wakefulness." On June 19, 2017,

Wambier died at home.

The newest armament proposal for South Korea is an American innovation, the THAAD missile defense system. The acronym stands for the Terminal High Altitude Area Defense. It is designed with "hit to kill" technology. It is capable of intercepting and destroying short- and intermediate-range missiles. Its capability has been well tested and successful. The US was anxious to place the weapons system in South Korea – missiles, along with radar, missile launchers, and control technology. It would protect South Korea from missile attacks from the North, and, importantly, protect the American military deployed there. In South Korea, former President Park became persuaded to approve the installation of the system in the ROK. It has been opposed by the People's Republic of China, one of South Korea's biggest trading partners, but because of the obvious energetic hostility expressed by Kim Jong Un, Park chose to favor that powerful form of protection for South Korea. Nevertheless, Park's partisan rivals in South Korea opposed this as another American intrusion into their foreign policy intensions.

An interesting international relations dynamic may accompany THAAD installations in South Korea. A significant reason for placing such weaponry in South Korea is to protect it from possible nuclear-armed missiles from the North. As the DPRK's brash Kim presses forward with both nuclear and missile tests, the presence of the US-ROK anti-missile system on the peninsula is perceived by China as a threat to its missile capabilities. In particular, the presence of the US radar technology that is part of THAAD would be introduced to South Korea and would compromise China's sense of its own military security. Such an increase of weaponry is perceived with concern by China as part of a larger containment policy on the part of the United States. If China can and does impose limits upon the DPRK, the rationale for the US enlargement of anti-missile weaponry in Asia is much reduced. China has leverage with the DPRK as its primary trading partner and immediate neighbor.

About eighty percent of North Korea's foreign trade is with China, and the United Nations' sanctions are squeezing other international traders. Most all of the DPRK's petroleum suppliers are from China (Leavenworth, *Christian Science Monitor*, May 11, 2016). Up to the present, China, as a matter of policy, has been reluctant to impose heavily upon its neighbor by making the United Nations' sanctions fully effective. Until recently, the poorly functioning customs officials at the China-North Korea border have made trade controls spotty at best and bribery is rampant (Perlez and Huang, *New York Times*, March 31, 2016).

The good news is there have been new moves in China to tighten controls on North Korea since the UN Security Council sanctions were strengthened on March 2, 2016. South Korean observers report that China has banned trade on sixty-five types of goods. Besides goods like iron ore, coal, and aviation fuel, "40 banned goods and technologies ... [that] can be used to make nuclear and biochemical weapons and missiles." It quoted experts, noting, "Chinese officials have made it clear that they intend to implement the [UN] resolution," as Beijing's response to heavy international pressure. The US State Department, emphasizing the United States' desire for a denuclearized DPRK, "welcomed China's agreement on the strongest sanctions Security Council has imposed in a generation" ("China bans...," *The Chosun Ilbo*, June 16, 2016).

In 2009, early in Obama's presidency, he declared as an urgent priority the prevention of more nuclear weapons in the world. Standing before a Nobel Peace Prize audience, he pointed the finger at Iran and North Korea. Subsequently, in 2015, he and the US State Department focused on Iran, eventually crafting an executive agreement with Iran to cease the development of weapons-grade nuclear material in exchange for relaxing a series of economic sanctions. The agreement survived a partisan rejection effort by congressional Republicans.

North Korean nuclear threats were dealt with by the Obama administration with what one critic called "an understated, almost leisurely, manner" (Kissinger, *New York Times*, June 3, 2009). In 2012, speaking in South Korea, Obama urged China to restrain North Korea regarding a space satellite. But the Obama administration chose not to take initiatives regarding a nuclear-armed North Korea. In a strikingly brash public provocation, the DPRK posted a video on YouTube (**www.youtube.com/watch?v=BrAZdnRAalo**) from the *DPRK Today*. North Korea has posted aggressive military scenes by North Korean forces and a simulated nuclear attack on Washington, DC. There have been other such North Korean postings showing Obama and the American troops on fire and Manhattan being bombed.

Provocations between the United States and North Korea did occur in July 2016 when the Obama administration took rhetorical action against President Kim and a dozen of his governing officials. The US State Department issued its "Report on Human Rights Abuses and Censorship in North Korea," thus holding Kim personally accountable for crimes against the human rights of North Korean people (US Department of State, July 6, 2016). Reporting to Congress, it cited findings by the United Nations Commission of Inquiry that reported "some of the most pervasive and notorious human rights abuses in the DPRK." Words in the report include "torture," "deliberate starvation," "sexual violence," "forced abortions," "surprise inspections in homes," and other kinds of abuse against persons. Acting on the report, the US imposed personal penalties upon Kim and his supporting cast of administrators. These sanctions froze financial assets in the US and outlawed business conducted with Americans. If lacking immediate bite, the sanctions publicized and personalized Kim's accountability to widely held standards of justice.

Unsurprisingly, the DPRK responded by closing a small, but previously used, diplomatic channel of communication with the US through UN officials for both countries. Considering the DPRK action both hostile and aggressive, South Korea's then President Park accepted the US military's request to deploy its newly developed THAAD missile defense installations at South Korean locations (Kim, for the Associated Press, July 11, 2016).

North Korea's militaristic moves did provoke tension from American presidential candidates Trump and Clinton in 2016. Trump's early comments on South Korea and Japan suggested they are too dependent on the US. He asserted that they should develop their own nuclear arsenals and that they should pay more for the presence of American troops. To influence China, he would threaten its access to American markets. After clinching the Republican presidential nomination, his views gained more scrutiny. In May 2016, Trump, who presents himself as a masterful deal maker, announced his willingness to meet with Kim Jong Un for negotiations about North Korea's nuclear resources and program. There were immediate criticisms from Democrats who noted that no American president has, while in office, dealt directly with any of the Kims. The argument is that such talks by Trump with Kim would unduly dignify the standing of this rising tyrant who has already been condemned for violating UN sanctions about weapons of mass destruction and is guilty of repressing thousands of innocent North Koreans in concentration camps.

South Korean media of responses to Trump's campaign rhetoric were negative as well. "It is scary just to imagine Trump, who often doesn't remember what he has said, getting elected president and manipulating Korean Peninsula issues by drastically shifting his positions," said a South Korean editorialist in May (quoted by Choe, *New York Times*, June 1, 2016). Meanwhile, the South Korean press noted the North Korean reception to Trump's candidacy. The North Korean *DPRK Today* website (which is based in China) praised Trump as a "wise politician" and "farsighted presidential candidate," even noting "Trump said he will not get involved in the war between the South and the North, isn't this fortunate from North Korea's perspective?" The South Korean response dismissed Trump's "ill-informed remarks that the US should stop paying for South Korea's defense" (*The Chosun Ilbo,* June 2, 2016).

Not surprisingly, Democrat Hillary Clinton tried to dismiss Trump's assertions regarding North Korea as reckless and uninformed, declaring Trump inadequately prepared for the tasks of diplomacy. But Trump, reckless or not, won the presidency and with it, the authority to reshape, perhaps radically, future relations with all the countries of Asia that have interests in the Korean Peninsula. An early clue that suggests what may turn into a rocky future is what Trump has said about himself: "I like to be unpredictable."

During most of the US presidential campaigns, the issues regarding China and the Koreas were mostly ignored by the candidates. Candidate Clinton was expected to continue Obama's patient posture toward North Korea. But the mostly unanticipated election of Donald Trump, whose comments about the issues regarding China, the United States, and the two Koreas have been suggestive, ambiguous, and far from definitive, have not yet produced clear policy directives by the US State and Defense Departments. What seems clear is that past patterns of foreign relations are likely to be shaken up in major ways and that the shifts will certainly affect the Korean Peninsula. Although initial exchanges between Trump and Russia's leader, Vladimir Putin, have raised controversy in the US and Europe, the relationships that the Trump administration forms with the Chinese leadership will likely set the parameters for how the US and the ROK respond to Kim and North Korea's provocations regarding nuclear weapons.

Keep in mind that North Korea is a threat taken with serious dread even by its primary ally, the People's Republic of China. Although what follows is speculation, it is a thoughtful commentary that comes from an informed source, *The Week*, an American news magazine. Its news analysis about the North Korean nuclear threat takes into account the array of consequences that Kim Jong Un's recklessness could bring, not only to North Korea but to China, South Korea, and the US. Thus it raises the consequential importance of the two Koreas to world affairs, an appropriate introduction to the remainder of this book.

Regime Collapse: The Aftermath

One of the biggest dilemmas China faces is trying to rein in its North Korean ally with economic sanctions — but without tipping Kim Jong Un's regime over the edge. If the regime collapses, experts agree, there will be absolute chaos. There would be widespread looting by the country's starving citizens, and violence in the gulags holding the country's 120,000 political prisoners. Millions of people would rush the border into China, and South Korean and U.S. troops would be forced to occupy a devastated and dysfunctional country. In his final days, Kim might choose to pass the nuclear weapons under his control to terrorists — or even launch them himself, as a final act of suicidal revenge. The regime's collapse would probably spark a brutal civil war with very high stakes, says North Korea expert Andrei Lankov — like "Syria with nukes" (*The Week*, August 5, 2016, p. 11).

One more complication to multinational efforts for preserving peace on the Korean Peninsula needs to be posted regarding a surprising political shift in South Korea. After a scandal publicized in October 2016, the National Assembly of the Republic of Korea voted in December 2016 to impeach President Park Geun Hye. Voting by secret ballot, 234 of the 300 members supported the action; half of the members of her own party were part of the overwhelming majority. Her crime was a conspiracy with a lifelong friend to extort great sums of money from several South Korean corporate enterprises. In South Korea, the impeachment charge had to be tried in the country's Constitutional Court. The Court unanimously convicted Park on March 10, 2017. With the South Korean presidency vacant, a special election was set for May. Moon Jae In, a human rights lawyer and political liberal, won the presidency. Moon proclaimed his opposition to American sanctions and pressure on North Korea. He even urged South Koreans to reach out to

North Koreans with the goal of peaceful reunification. Moon also has decried the United States' THAAD weaponry, but has not removed emplacements brought into South Korea before Moon's election. It remains to be seen how South Korea's newly softened approach to North Korea's hostility will affect negotiating positions of President Xi of China and the emerging foreign policy of the Trump administration in the US. So far, Trump has talked tough about relationships in Asia, but, on the other hand, indicated willingness to open direct negotiations with North Korea. Moreover, after his first visit with China's President Xi in February 2017, Trump expressed great regard and respect for Xi, exuding confidence that they can work together toward resolving tensions in all of Korea.

To summarize, judging from recent events in Korea, one can recognize that a hostile regime in North Korea has built up a small but lethal nuclear weapons program to back up its unique "go it alone" *Juche* version of communism. The DPRK leadership believes its weapons of mass destruction assure it immunity from control by the United Nations, and particularly the Republic of Korea and the United States. There have been historic peace initiatives to reconcile North and South Korea since the war in 1950-1953, but the enthusiasm for that long-delayed solution has suffered a large decline. But the ROK's newly elected President Moon wants to reverse that decline. The key international participants affecting the twentieth and twenty-first century history of the ROK and the DPRK have been China, the United States, Japan, and Russia (formerly the Soviet Union). The Republic of Korea has prospered with its thoroughly capitalistic economy and a hard won, successfully functioning democracy. The so-called Democratic People's Republic of Korea, which is not at all democratic, endures as a dark and dismal impoverished nation under an exploitative communistic tyrant. The two halves of the Korean Peninsula have developed very differently in the more than seventy years since the two separate governing systems were put in place in 1946. This book will elaborate on those separate developments. After that, I will consider what may be prescient judgments and forecasts about the future of South and North Korea.

CHAPTER I: THE KOREAN PROBLEM

The Korean Peninsula is a distinctive mountainous extension of the Asian continent. As seen on the globe, it appears almost suspended from the eastern end of the Asian mainland. It has a huge neighbor to the north: China. Yet its northeastern border touches Russia. East across the sea is the country of Japan. Korea and its people have long been buffeted and limited by the forces and personalities generated in its larger neighbors. But Koreans, a distinctive people, have resisted domination from the grasping neighbors who have challenged Korean independence. For Americans to get a sense of location, the northeastern-most extension of Korea is at the 43rd parallel, and its southern-most point is close to the 34th parallel. To compare, San Diego lies close to the 34th parallel and Salem, Oregon, is at the 44th parallel. The Korean Peninsula extends nearly seven hundred miles from south to north.

During what was the Dark Ages of Western history and civilization, the Korean Peninsula was home to three kingdoms. The northern one was called Koguyo. In the southwest was Paekche, but Silla, in the southeast, became dominant, conquering the others. A new dynasty arose in the 10th century that achieved greater national unity and is known as the Koryo kingdom. It endured into the 14th century. After that, the Choson Dynasty maintained a degree of national unity despite challenges from China, the Mongolian Empire, and Japan. A serious attack on Korea was initiated by Japan near the end of the 16th century, but a still renowned Korean Admiral, Yi Sun Shin, defeated the Japanese invaders in a series of naval battles. Nevertheless, during the 17th century, the Koreans became tributaries of the Qing Dynasty in China. China and Japan continued as rivals in their desires to control Korea well into the 19th century.

In what historians reference as the First Sino-Japanese War, beginning in 1894, Japan defeated the Chinese in a land battle at Pyongyang, then Korea's capital, and in a naval fight at the Yalu River. China then withdrew its forces from Korea, but the relentless Japanese pursued them on land and sea, defeating both Chinese naval and army forces. When the Japanese threatened Beijing, China sued for peace. After the conflict, the 1895 settlement arrived at was known as the Treaty of Shimonoseki. According to the treaty, China let go of Korea and Japan assumed its control as a "protectorate." Japan's military success heightened recognition of the country as a major world power and it revealed the weakness and decline of the Qing Dynasty's control over all of China (Ferguson and Bruun, p. 873).

The Korean social structure when Japan began its domination was rigid and hierarchical. A small *yangban* elite constituted its ruling class. Under a monarch, the elite dominated the political system and its governmental positions. Trained and educated functionaries, clerks, and professionals constituted a small middle class. The common people consisted of artisans, tradesmen, and mostly farmers. Employment in the middle and lower class was determined by heredity. Except for the elite, most people had little expectation about occupational or locational mobility. The Korean people were united by a distinctive language. Its tradition of Confucianism regulated relations between husbands and wives, fathers and sons, and, importantly, ruler and ruled.

Japan's economic needs for raw materials and agricultural products, especially rice, made Korea a prime takeover target. In 1902, Japan entered into an alliance with Great Britain, the world's foremost sea power, giving Japan increased international standing. Japan would respect Britain's interest in China in return for Britain's acknowledgment of Japanese stakes in Korea. Both countries regarded Russian aspirations in China, particularly Manchuria, and Korea as threats of intrusion. Japan acted upon its enmity for Russia in 1904 in the Russo-Japanese War. Russia had coerced a lease of the Liaodong Peninsula (northwest of Korea) from the Chinese, providing czarist Russia with a warm water port, Port Arthur, in the Yellow Sea. Protected by 50,000 Russian soldiers, the Japanese brought an army of 90,000 to the attack. Casualties were high on both sides, the Russians losing 60,000 soldiers to Japan's loss of 41,000. The Japanese destroyed much of the Russian naval force. Thereupon the Japanese asked the US president, then Theodore Roosevelt, to negotiate a peace agreement, remembered as the Treaty of Portsmouth. The agreement, with American approval, gave Japan control of Korea and much of southern Manchuria, including Port Arthur (Ferguson and Bruun, p. 878).

In 1905, Japan gained acceptance of its interests in Korea by a treaty involving the US and occupied Korea in a major way. Upon achieving solid control five years later, Japan annexed Korea in the Japan-Korea Treaty of 1910 without objection from the world's leading nations. With an imposing cultural invasion, Japan took effective command of the instruments of government and established a military rule of colonialism in Korea. Japanese immigrants were installed into the governing bureaucracy. Indigenous Koreans were kept in place, engaged mostly in agriculture. The Japanese redefined land ownership laws and over time, most of the productive farmland was recognized as the property of the Japanese. The Korean countryside became the source of needed rice and raw materials for the Japanese homeland.

Japan invested in Korean infrastructure – roads, electrical power production, railways, and various modes of communication (a modern postal system, radio, telegraph and telephone media). During the 1930s, the Japanese developed manufacturing and chemical industries, tapping into the coal, iron, and other mineral wealth especially available in northern Korea. This modernization of Korea was brought about by Japanese capital and industrial ingenuity, while Koreans provided the farmers, tradesmen, and factory workers. Consumption of Korean products was mostly the privilege of the Japanese in Korea and in their homeland. Under harsh Japanese rule, Koreans benefited little from the results of modernization. In 1937, the Japanese rulers sought to replace the Korean language with Japanese. School students were to use the language not only in school but outside as well. Korean-language newspapers disappeared and many Koreans took Japanese names. As Japan enlarged its military, it began to enlist Korean volunteers into its armed forces in 1938. During World War II, Korean youths were drafted into the Japanese army but the war did not materially touch the Korean Peninsula. By the war's end, nearly two and a half million Koreans were in Japan to bolster its war production efforts. Notoriously, thousands of young Korean women were forced to be "comfort women" — in effect, sex slaves for the Japanese military. Many Koreans, used as forced laborers, never returned to their native country. The exploitation of the Koreans by the Japanese stimulated internal resistance, taking the form of boycotts of Japanese goods, labor strikes, and student demonstrations. To this day, there remains, among many Koreans in both the North and the South, a bitter sense of resentment against the Japanese (Savada and Shaw, 1992).

Japan's abrupt World War II surrender on August 15, 1945, left a peculiar vacuum of rulership in Korea. The prevailing major powers - the USSR, Britain, and the US - had many concerns to settle, mostly with regard to Germany, Eastern Europe, China, and Japan. Consequential decisions had already been hammered out by the leaders of the Allied victors with provisions for Korea almost an afterthought. In November 1943, at the Cairo Conference, a minor point was recorded that "in due course, Korea shall become free and independent." A more concrete proposal from President Franklin D. Roosevelt at the Yalta Conference in February 1945 to the Soviets was for Korea to be held as a trusteeship under China, the USSR, and the US for as long as twenty or thirty years. With the war against Japan still raging, Roosevelt solicited Stalin with an incentive to provide military help in completing the defeat of the Japanese.

By the summer of 1945, Germany had surrendered and the USSR was moving troops to Asia. American atomic bombs brought Japan to its knees. President Harry S. Truman's advisers now feared the Soviet entry into northern China (Manchuria) could become an intrusion into the whole Korean Peninsula. Thereupon, the United States, recognizing a possible threat to all its Asian interests, had to decide how to face the Soviet Union regarding Korea. According to Don Oberdorfer, the action went like this:

> On the evening of August 10, 1945, with Tokyo suing for peace and Soviet troops on the move, an all-night meeting was convened in the Executive Office Building next to the White House to decide what to do about accepting the impending Japanese surrender in Korea and elsewhere in Asia. Around midnight two young officers were sent into an adjoining room to carve out a US occupation zone in Korea, lest the Soviets occupy the entire peninsula and move quickly toward Japan. Lieutenant Colonels Dean Rusk, who was later to be secretary of state under Presidents Kennedy and Johnson, and Charles Bonesteel, who was later US military commander in Korea, had little preparation for the task. Working in haste and under great pressure, and using a *National Geographic* map for reference, they proposed that US troops occupy the area south of the thirty-eighth parallel, which was approximately halfway up the peninsula and north of the city of Seoul, and that Soviet troops occupy the area north of the parallel.

No Korean experts were involved in the decision
...

> The thirty-eighth-parallel line was hastily incor-
> porated into General Order Number One for the
> occupation of Japanese-held territory. Despite the
> fact that US forces were far away and would not
> arrive on the scene for several weeks, the Soviets
> carefully stopped their southward advance at the
> parallel. Thus, Korea came to be divided into two
> "temporary" zones of occupation that, as the Cold
> War deepened, became the sites of two antag-
> onistic Korean regimes based on diametrically
> opposed principles and sponsors (Oberdorfer and
> Carlin, p.5).

The division of the Korean Peninsula into roughly two
halves was, as noted, done without specialized knowledge
from Korean policy experts. Moreover, it was done without
input by any Korean leaders. If there was a consensus
among Korean people, it was about an expectation that
there should be only one government for the entire peninsula. At the time, autumn of 1945, there was a pragmatic
understanding between the US and the USSR that each
would oversee half of the peninsula until a single governing
arrangement could be formulated and established.

In the southern portion of the peninsula, the job of
occupation fell primarily to the US Army. Neither it nor the
State Department possessed much expertise about Korea.
Except for some Christian missionaries, few Americans had
any on-the-ground understanding about Korean culture and
society. There was little clarity in Washington about where
and how a Korean nation would find a peaceful place among
the countries of its region and the larger world. Although not
a war torn locale in the sense that many countries were at
that time, Korea was underdeveloped, poor, and its people
were inexperienced in home rule.

General John R. Hodge was assigned to command a US
occupational army. His task was to apply his army to the

goal of bringing about "the establishment of a free and independent nation." Arriving in Korea in September 1945, with little knowledge about the people or the culture, Hodge discovered a couple of groupings of Koreans were organizing to claim control of an indigenous government. There were streams of Korean exiles coming from abroad, mostly China, some from Japan, and even a noteworthy few from the United States. Not surprisingly, an already formed and rather popular Korean Communist Party was developing a following among the working people and students. Hodge and the Americans suspiciously perceived that as a political force directed from the Soviet Union via Pyongyang. The Americans would not recognize any claims from Koreans to leadership. In the meantime, hated by the Koreans, the Japanese functionaries largely departed the country's administrative and corporate positions. An increasingly unpopular direct rule by the American military, unskilled in Korean language and culture, sought to impose order while waiting for the establishment of a multinational trusteeship to run the country. However, there was "economic distress and political turmoil in the American zone" (Matray, p. 19). Koreans in the south, both those on the political right and the left, opposed the proposed trusteeship that would subject the nation to outside leaders. Koreans wanted Korean leadership. The Americans were regarded as not much better than the Japanese rulers before them.

The economy in the south was not functioning very well given the departure of the previous Japanese managers. Returning Korean exiles were crowding into Seoul and other southern, urban places. Unemployment was high. Most of the factories and mines were in the Soviet zone, and those resources were not accessible to the people in the south. Early on, the Russians stopped mail, railroad lines, and delivery of resources such as coal and industrial products from easy transport from the north to the south. The electrical grid, mostly powered in the north, was often interrupted in the south. Meanwhile, the USSR was establishing a Soviet bloc in eastern Europe. In March 1946,

Winston Churchill warned the Western allies that "an iron curtain has descended across the [European] Continent." The boundary of separation in Korea came to be viewed as an extension of that Iron Curtain. The American occupiers more and more sensed a threat from communist organizers in the south, and therefore were biased in favor of business owners and those wanting a capitalistic economy for the support of a democratic government. There were unsuccessful negotiations in 1946 and 1947 between the US and the USSR about Korea's future. The US was arguing for elections in both the north and the south so that Koreans could form a government for the entire peninsula. Unable to come to an agreement, the US chose to hand off the problem in September 1947 to the United Nations.

The Soviet occupation of Korea north of the 38th parallel proceeded a great deal more successfully than its American counterpart effort in the south (Jager, p. 19). If the Soviet army was no more sophisticated than the US military, its leadership could and did draw upon ethnic Koreans who were Soviet citizens and committed communists. Many of those ethnic Koreans had departed their homeland during the Japanese occupation. They were on the Bolshevik side in the Russian Civil War. They were aligned with the Russians and the Nationalist Chinese as enemies of Japan during World War II. Stalin could and did recruit these ethnic Koreans, including military veterans who were willing communist loyalists, to help occupy and operate in the Soviet-controlled north. "With Soviet Koreans working directly with the populace, Soviet authorities were able to control their zone unobtrusively while promoting Soviet policies" (Jager, p. 23). So the Soviet military effectively oversaw a bureaucracy that was largely staffed by imported Korean loyalists who, like good soldiers, dependably carried out the military's purposes. Direction at the top came from General Nicolai Lebedev, who headed the Soviet Civil Administration (SCA), and General Terentii Fomich Shtykov, who negotiated with the United States on behalf of the Soviets. The latter would become the first

Soviet ambassador to North Korea. A political officer, he had access to Stalin and expertise about Korea. He was a major player in turning Moscow's policy wishes in Korea's northern sector into operational programs.

By the end of 1945, the SCA required activist citizen groups to register their members. The SCA could thereby distinguish potential supporters and resisters to the collectivist directions coming from the Soviet leadership. This prompted some grassroots opposition that was addressed with heavy-handed military enforcement for the SCA's intentions. As word spread among the people, a stream of dissident refugees, including many Christian Koreans, began to move from the north into the American zone. According to news reports in the US, by mid-1947, the count of people from the north to the south was nearly two million (*New York Times*, July 9, 1947). As far as the Soviets were concerned, such movement was not resisted. For them, it effectively reduced the presence of dissident voices and political opponents, easing progress toward the new regime's purposes.

In the south, the Americans were dealing clumsily with the turbulence brought by a weak economy, an influx of refugee Koreans, and polarizing political groups on the political right and left. The Soviets helped foment political conflict in the south by providing financial support to the South Korean Workers' Party. Fruitless negotiations between the USSR and the US about forming a trusteeship for all of Korea produced frustration among the Soviets as well as the Americans. In September 1947, the Soviet negotiator Shtykov boldly offered to have the Soviet military withdraw from the north in 1948 if the US would likewise withdraw its troops. In effect, he argued, let the Koreans work out their own governing arrangements. The Soviets judged that their better organized people could likely prevail in a Koreans-only decision process. The US's response was, as noted above, to ask the United Nations to deal with the problem.

The UN acted with dispatch. On November 17, 1947, the General Assembly passed a resolution to set up a UN Temporary Commission on Korea (UNTCOK). Its assignment was to supervise free elections in Korea, assist in the withdrawal of American and Soviet occupying forces and assist in the creation of a Korean government. The UN scheduled elections in May 1948 for a representative assembly. The assembly would then choose a president. The Soviets chose not to allow the commission admission to the north to conduct an election, but the US welcomed the initiative, anxious to rid itself of the burdens of dealing with squabbling among Koreans and other problems.

An election process was put in place in the south only, overseen by the UN, and it created the south's constitutional assembly. There were nearly eight million voters who elected two hundred assembly members on May 10, 1948. Nominally, there were six separate parties that elected one hundred and five of the members, fifty-five of which were chosen under the party name National Alliance for the Rapid Realization of Korean Independence. Another ninety-five members were mostly independents. The election took place amid great controversy, particularly by those who saw the election as a barrier to unification of the Korean Peninsula as one nation. The resulting National Assembly of South Korea reserved one hundred seats for the eventually expected members from the north.

The political response in the north was its own elections resulting in the Supreme People's Assembly in North Korea on August 25, 1948. The Korean Workers' Party (KWP) allowed one candidate per constituency and produced an assembly of 572 members. A provisional arrangement was made to eventually include 360 members from the south.

On July 17, 1948, the South Korean Constitutional Assembly adopted its constitution. One of the persons elected to that body was Syngman Rhee. Rhee became the National Assembly's choice for president on July 20, 1948. He received 180 votes out of 196 cast in the Assembly. The Republic of Korea (ROK) declared its independence as a constitutional government of all Korea on August 15, 1948. The date was three years to the day after Japanese occupation of the peninsula ended in 1945.

In Pyongyang, the Supreme People's Assembly proclaimed itself the Democratic People's Republic of Korea (DPRK), adopted its constitution, and declared its independence on September 8, 1948. Its prime minister, Kim Il Sung, announced in October that the DPRK would make "every effort to realize ... the unification of the Fatherland" (Wada, p. 3). Two constitutionally established governments, one on each side of the 38th parallel, had each now proclaimed itself the legitimate government of the Korean Peninsula. Each regime expressed as its goal the task of unifying a single nation. Leaders on both sides were of a mind to remove the other by whatever means were necessary. The next two years would be marked by provocations by each side upon the other. However, the two Korean regimes were constrained by the occupation forces of their great power protectors, the United States and the Soviet Union, who were increasing rivals in the world's developing Cold War.

In January 1949, Kim Il Sung wanted to cement his and the DPRK's relations with Stalin's Soviet Union. Kim needed to find out how firm and generous Stalin's support would be should the DPRK make a move against the ROK. Kim's request to Soviet Ambassador Shtykov was for Kim to have a much-needed face-to-face meeting with Stalin. In March 1949, Kim led a seven-member DPRK delegation, getting direct access to Stalin, the world leader of the communist movement. Kim's line of argument was that the anti-communists in the ROK were preventing any negotiation that might unite Korea until the ROK developed the strength to attack the DPRK. Kim, fearful of the strengthening ROK and judging his side as the stronger, wanted to attack first. Despite concluding a cooperative agreement with Kim regarding economic and technological assistance, along with some military support and training, Stalin told Kim that he opposed a DPRK invasion. Stalin judged that the DPRK was not clearly superior to the ROK and that an attack would cause the United States to intervene.

There were provocative acts by the ROK along the 38th parallel in early 1949. ROK police units attacked various

DPRK police centers. According to Soviet intelligence, there were thirty-seven border incursions by the South, mostly between March 15 and April 15 (Wada, p. 15). It is unclear whether or not these were coordinated incursions or acts led by local police commanders. Of more serious concern in the South were attacks by local communists on the police and community government officials. An intense challenge came on the southern island of Cheju-do between April 1948 and June 1949. After Rhee assumed the ROK presidency, there was a "reign of terror largely perpetrated by government forces, the police and the Republic of Korea Army (ROKA)" "[A]n estimated thirty thousand have been killed in Cheju-do, many of them innocent civilians massacred by government forces" (Jager, pp. 51 and 53).

During the years between 1945 and 1950, while the Soviets and Americans could not forge a unified plan for Korea and rival forces within were threatening each other with aggression, much was changing in the rest of the world (for a larger discussion see Sheehan, pp. 49-114). Already the Soviets were assisting the formation of communist governments in eastern Europe. By contrast, in 1946, the US yielded independence to the Philippines on July 4, 1946. In March 1947, US President Harry S. Truman announced what is remembered as the Truman Doctrine: the US would support true democracies around the world and resist the growth of communist regimes. In 1947, Secretary of State George Marshall presented the idea of massive economic aid to western European countries devastated by World War II. It became known as the Marshall Plan and was adopted by Congress in 1948 and implemented thereafter. In 1948, a communist coup in Czechoslovakia brought an extension of the Soviet Union's Iron Curtain into central Europe. The Soviets established the Berlin Blockade in January 1948, which was successfully resisted by an airlift of goods by the Western Allies until the blockade was lifted in May 1949. In August 1949, the Soviets successfully tested an atomic bomb, putting the Western powers on notice about nuclear parity. The US's strategy of containment of the Soviet Union led to the formation of a mutual defense treaty and the North Atlantic Treaty Organization (NATO), comprised of ten European nations with the US and Canada in 1949. In Asia, colonial regimes of France and the Netherlands were breaking down. A civil war between the Nationalist Chinese, led by Chiang Kai-shek, and Communist China, led by Mao Zedong, resulted in the collapse of the Nationalists and the withdrawal of that regime to the island of Formosa (Taiwan). On October 1, 1949, Mao declared the organization of the People's Republic of China (PRC). Meanwhile, the US was seeking to organize a democratic regime in Japan as an ally and a bulwark against communist encroachment in Asia. Eventually, a treaty of peace was concluded in 1951. In Korea, the Soviet military did withdraw from the DPRK in the autumn of 1948. The US responded, removing all but a small core of military advisers in July 1949. By 1950, the next moves regarding nationhood in Korea seemed to be left to the prudence, or lack thereof, by the rival regimes in the north and the south of the Korean Peninsula. For the US, that was the essence of the Korean problem.

In January 1950, Kim Il Sung was still seeking to renew his request to the Soviet Union that the DPRK be supported in an attack on the ROK. After a controversial speech in the US by Secretary of State Dean Atchison that omitted Korea from inclusion within the "defensive perimeter ... of US military forces," Stalin informed Kim about his willingness to support the DPRK's desire to attack the ROK. "[O] n February 9, Stalin promised that the CPSU [Communist Party of the Soviet Union] Central Committee would favorably consider North Korea's loan request [70,700,000 rubles annually for three years, for North Korea a vast sum], approval of the formation of three KPA [Korean People's Army] divisions, and payment of the 1951 credit allocation in 1950 ... Kim Il-sung was deliriously happy" (Wada, p. 55). It was Kim's intention to achieve Korean unification by force. Stalin promised support, but not direct participation in the conflict. Moreover, his approval was conditional upon Mao's support. Stalin required Kim to solicit Chinese help from Mao Zedong, who "promised all-out support for Kim Il Sung's attempt to unify Korea, including Chinese forces if Washington entered the fighting" (Wada, p. 61). True to his word, Mao sent Kim two divisions of China's People's Liberation Army (PLA) consisting of Koreans who fought the Japanese in China during World War II.

In the American zone, the US ambassador to the ROK, John Muccio, judged that after the withdrawal of Soviet and American armies, the forces on both sides of the 38th parallel were about evenly balanced and that neither side would "in the foreseeable future assume the risks associated with a deliberate all-out invasion" (Wada, p. 26). The American military's Joint Chiefs of Staff went on record saying that "Korea is of little strategic value to the United States and that any commitment to the United States use of military force in Korea would be ill-advised and impracticable" (Wada, p. 29). Meanwhile, the ROK president, Syngman Rhee, entered one-on-one negotiations with Chiang Kai Shek about mutual assistance and resistance against communist moves against either government or both. Reportedly, Chiang offered air support to the ROK in case of an invasion by the South against the North (Wada, p. 31). By 1950, the ROK economy was suffering an inflationary spiral. The ROK military, suspecting an invasion from the DPRK, developed a plan for withdrawal as necessary until the DPRK's army became overstretched and could be counterattacked. In the South Korean legislative elections in May 1950, the political results favored President Rhee's rivals. Prospects for governmental consensus in problem solving regarding challenging issues both domestic and military appeared to be tenuous. Despite signs that the DPRK was assembling military forces close to the 38th parallel, on June 1, 1950, President Truman reassured Americans that the world was "closer to peace than at any time in the last five years" (Jager, p. 63). Needless to say, that was not an apt prophecy. Shortly later, John Foster Dulles, then in the State Department, addressed the ROK National Assembly on June 19, 1950, encouraging them to believe that although the US had no treaty obligation to defend the ROK, the US would respond to defend freedom in the world against "unprovoked military aggression." "South Koreans interpreted the speech as a guarantee of their security" (Wada, pp.69-70). The mix of strategies and faulty opinions on the American side was ripe for an impending disaster.

CHAPTER 2: GOING TO WAR IN KOREA

Near the end of June 1950, the Democratic People's Republic of Korea (DPRK) massed most of its troops, the Korean People's Army (KPA), including 258 tanks, close to the boundary between the North and South. Its engineers dismantled their own minefields, which protected the North from attack by the South, in order to allow its own troops to safely proceed through cleared lanes into South Korea. The DPRK's attack began in the early morning of June 25, using several jumping off points along the 38th parallel. The next day, Kim Il Sung publicly lied to the world, declaring that the North was responding to an attack from the South. He claimed, "We are waging a just war for unification and independence of the fatherland, freedom and democracy." He blamed the "puppet forces of the traitor Syngman Rhee." However, documentary discoveries since the war show that Soviet Ambassador Shtykov carefully and accurately reported the North's initiative to Moscow on June 26 (Wada, pp. 75-78). The undeclared attack successfully threw the Republic of Korea's (ROK) forces into chaos and retreat. By June 28, the ROK capital of Seoul was captured and DPRK forces were moving rapidly south.

As the attackers advanced, the DPRK's leaders called upon the citizenry of the South to join the North and become part of a single national movement. Their appeal was enter into a communist revolution that would unify Korea as a single nation. In occupied Seoul, the DPRK's political leaders required political parties to register with the new regime, promising that they would "sweep away the traitors" and soon occupy all of the South (Wada, pp. 80-81). As the KPA successfully advanced militarily, the DPRK's political cadres moved in to organize "People's Committees" in the cities and the towns. Claiming that they were acting according to provisions in the DPRK Constitution, the invading government confiscated land from the owners and began a redistribution effort to farmers and tenants. The public effect was to curry favor with the neediest people. The Rhee regime and its supporters were everywhere, condemned as lackeys of the US and enemies of the people.

The ROK Army was ill-equipped to defend against the North's tanks and small air force. The Americans had deliberately denied Rhee's army from having heavy artillery, tanks, and antitank weapons lest the frisky Rhee actually attack first. "Faced by an assault of such formidable power and decision, Syngman Rhee's army was wholly unable to mount a coherent defense by formations. Reeling, its battered and broken companies began to struggle southward, often abandoning their equipment, hastening to keep a brief bound ahead of the bleak, mustard-drab battalions of Kim Il Sung's victorious army" (Hastings, p. 53).

A particular effort was made by the ROK to stop the North at the Han River, south of Seoul. However, that effort failed. The KPA was effectively knifing its way through the ROK troops like butter. "After one week of war, Syngman Rhee's army could account for only 54,000 of its men. The remaining 44,000 had merely disappeared, many of them never to be seen again" (Hastings, p. 73). Quickly, alarm bells went off in Washington. American Ambassador Muccio notified the State Department that this was a major act of war. Secretary of State Acheson promptly issued a call for the United Nations to order a ceasefire. June 25 was a Sunday. President Truman and others were away from Washington. The UN Security Council did enact a ceasefire resolution. At the time, the Soviets were boycotting the UN sessions because the Nationalist Chinese were UN members, not the People's Republic of China. Over the next several days, President Truman, Secretary of State Acheson, the military top brass, and leaders of Congress conducted rounds of talk. By Friday, June 30, President Truman authorized General Douglas MacArthur, commander of American forces in Asia, to send a regimental combat team, then in Japan, to begin a buildup of American forces in Korea. In a cautious judgment, the president turned down an offer of troops by the Nationalist Chinese, deciding instead to approve the authorization for two American divisions from Japan to follow the regimental combat team. The secretary of state summed up his description of events saying, "Friday's decisions where the culminating ones of a momentous week. We were then fully committed in Korea" (Acheson, p. 413).

By the end of the first week of July, the United States had its 24th Division, previously based in Japan, on the ground in South Korea. This occupational force from Japan was hardly a deadly threat to stop the DPRK's well-prepared attackers. "Their unit, like all those of the Occupation Army in Japan, was badly understrength and poorly equipped" (Hastings, p. 16). But, despite their limitations, these were the closest American forces, about 15,000 in number. They had to play the part of vanguard for a larger contingent yet to come. Hastings reports that during the first seventeen days of the 24th's action, it had "lost some 30 percent of their strength, more than 2,400 men missing in action" (Hastings, p. 80). It quickly became known that the attackers were ruthless with prisoners, when surrendered Americans, hands tied behind their backs, were shot dead and left on a roadside (Hastings, p. 81). The North's army was willing to engage in human wave charges against the bewildered defenders. American withdrawals sometimes turned into panic, with GIs throwing down arms and running away. Despite these failings, however, "the North Koreans suffered some 58,000 casualties between June 25 and early August" (Hastings, p. 82). By the end of that awful month, the beleaguered Americans and their

ROK comrades were able to halt the DPRK advance and solidify a defense at what became known as the Pusan Perimeter. There, the American field commander, General Walton "Bulldog" Walker, could reinforce his mauled army. They withstood forays throughout August 31, when the KPA gave its advance one more furious effort. Walker's forces stood fast. "The Communists had reached the limits of men, guns, supplies, ammunition. The Pusan Perimeter held" (Hastings, p. 98).

During the desperate days of retreat by the Allies, General Douglas MacArthur, the Supreme Commander for the United Nations' forces, was not idle. He and his staff conceived a plan to make a risky amphibious landing on the west coast of the peninsula, adjacent to Seoul, at a place called Inchon. It is well to take note of Commander MacArthur, seventy years old, and the senior and most notable serving American general of that time. His military record dated back to World War I. He had been the Army Chief of Staff before World War II. He was commander in chief of the Army's Pacific forces during that war. With the outbreak of conflict in Korea, all the allied forces were under his command. His brilliance as a bold commander and superb strategist was widely recognized and praised, but his reputation included a critical concern about his ego. "Throughout his life he acted on the assumption that the rules made for lesser men had no relevance to himself" (Hastings, p. 65). Also noted about MacArthur

> was the immense amount of energy he had always put into making sure that his image was the proper one, that he got the maximum amount of credit for any victory, while his subordinates received as little credit as possible. He was the most theatrical of men, busy at all times not merely being a general but doing it in the most dramatic way possible, the Great MacArthur who played in nothing less than the theater of history – as if life were always a stage and the world his audience (Halberstam, p. 103).

The Inchon invasion was boldly conceived. The tricky thirty foot tides could make the muddy landing area a quagmire for invading troops, and the hills beyond could allow defenders advantageous fields of fire. Despite the arguments from others about the risks, MacArthur pitched the challenge and the opportunity. "He asserted the very implausibility of his own plan as its strongest argument for surprise, and thus success" (Hastings p. 102). The American Joint Chiefs of Staff (JCS) approved the operation. MacArthur chose his own chief of staff, Major General Edward Almond, to be in command of X Corps, the landing force. The landings began on September 15, 1950. The perilous possibilities regarding tides and weather did not stop the invaders and the North Koreans mounted no counterattack.

> Astoundingly, two regiments were established ashore in Inchon at a cost of just 20 killed among a total of less than 200 casualties. If the landing on the west coast of Korea was a makeshift, amateurish affair ... it had proved formidable enough to overcome the primitive legions of Kim Il Sung. In the days that followed, as the men of the 7th Division and the 7th Marines followed the vanguard ashore, MacArthur and his officers exulted. The gamble had triumphantly succeeded. All the Supreme Commander's instincts about the conduct of the North Koreans had been justified (Hastings, p. 109).

Following the invasion, there was a bitter battle for the capital city of Seoul, prosecuted by American Marines supported with stunningly effective artillery and air support. On September 29, MacArthur ceremoniously proclaimed the liberation of Seoul and, with "a characteristic flood of rhetoric," turned the civil control of the city to President Rhee (Hastings, p. 114). "For MacArthur, success of the Inchon plan and the liberation of Seoul were both the vindication and a professional triumph ... His honor and reputation had been strengthened to epic proportions. He saved South Korea" (Jaeger, p. 83). With his reputation never higher and his ego beyond self-doubt, MacArthur would shortly over-reach himself.

On the North Korean side, Kim Il Sung had to acknowledge his army's grave circumstances. The KPA had exhausted itself at the Pusan Perimeter. The ROK and the American Eighth Army broke out on the attack, while the success in Seoul allowed a cutoff of North Korean troops fleeing the breakout at the Pusan Perimeter. On September 29, 1950, Kim wrote a beseeching letter to Stalin. He acknowledged that the Allies' "thousand airplanes ... totally dominate the airspace ... [T]he assault force that landed in Inchon with the units of their southern front that broke through our front line, the adversary has a real opportunity to take over the city of Seoul completely. As a result, the units of the People's Army that are still fighting in the southern part of Korea have been cut off from the northern part of Korea, they are torn into pieces." After reassuring Stalin that his forces would fight "to the last drop of blood," he asked that "when enemy troops cross over the 38th parallel we will badly need direct military assistance from the Soviet Union." Moreover, "please assist us by forming international volunteer units in China and other countries of people's democracy for rendering military assistance in our struggle" (Wada, pp. 117-118).

Even before the Inchon invasion, there was optimism in Washington about a UN breakout. If it was success-ful, what next? In the American State Department there were two views. "One was that under no circumstances should General MacArthur's forces cross the 38th paral-lel" (Atchison, p. 445). Although that would have been a clear policy decision, a variety of arguments was supposed against it, but not an obvious alternative policy. Atchison described the situation this way:

> One conclusion was clear: no arbitrary prohibition against crossing the parallel should be imposed. As a boundary it had no political validity. The next most important conclusion was not clear. After knocking out the invasion and as much of the

invasion force as seemed practical, what then? The official United Nations purpose was to create a unified, independent, and democratic Korea. But how and by whom? These were words and empty words; they were not policy. One of our greatest problems lay in ever getting beyond them (Atchison, p. 445).

It turned out that President Truman and his secretary of state were not able to control the policy decision and its implementation. In particular, ROK President Rhee publicly announced that his ROK forces would not stop at the 38th parallel, but would continue the attack on the North. After success at Inchon, the American Joint Chiefs, with the agreement of the president and the State Department, gave MacArthur permission to operate north of the 38th parallel, but required that he clear his plans with the Joint Chiefs. Instead, MacArthur took command prerogatives. Atchison reports that "General MacArthur, without warning or notice to Washington, ordered his commanders to 'drive forward with all speed and full utilization of their forces.' The restraining line in the north was thus abolished and with it the inhibition against other than South Korean troops in the border provinces." MacArthur claimed the rationale that "the mission of the UN force is to clear Korea" (Atchison, p. 462). Then, MacArthur made the mistake of dividing his commanders. The Eighth Army, under General Walker, proceeded north on the western side of the peninsula. The X Corps, under Almond, moved up along the eastern side of the peninsula. Both forces were themselves divided into separate columns, racing forward without effective means of coordination, but not opposed by a well-formed opposition. In the middle of October, having given assurances to President Truman that the Chinese would not attack his forces, MacArthur forecast that resistance would be over by Thanksgiving and he would even withdraw forces in time for Christmas (Hastings pp. 121-122). According to Atchison:

On November 17 MacArthur had informed the Chiefs that on the twenty-fourth he would start a general offensive to attain the line of the Yalu. His air attacks had isolated the battlefield from enemy reinforcements. While the supply situation was unsatisfactory, he nevertheless proposed to clear the country of enemy forces before the Yalu froze and furnished a crossing for overwhelming numbers. Such was the reasoning. A cautionary cable from the Chiefs of Staff urging him to stop on the high ground commanding the Yalu Valley was brushed aside as 'utterly impossible.' In the full optimism of that manic tide he flew to the Eighth Army headquarters on the Chongchon River and proclaimed the general offensive in the northwest, declaring, 'If successful this should for all practical purposes end the war, restore peace and unity to Korea, enable the prompt withdrawal of United Nations military forces, and permit the complete assumption by the Korean people and the nation of full sovereignty and international equality' (Atchison, pp. 467-468).

What McArthur did not know and what his chief of intelligence Major General Charles A. Willoughby refused to believe is that Mao had committed a huge, but undetected, Chinese military force in North Korea. An initial small army of Chinese engaged Americans near the Chosin Reservoir, then withdrew into the hills and forests nearby. In what was an extraordinarily successful and largely secretive move, a large force of Chinese ventured across the Yalu River into North Korea.

Between October 13 and 20 the intelligence staffs of MacArthur's armies failed to discern the slightest evidence of the movement of 130,000 soldiers and porters. A combination of superb fieldcraft and camouflage by the Chinese, with their lack of use of any of the conventional means of detecting modern military movement – wireless traffic, mechanized activity, supply dumps – blinded the UN Command to what was taking place on its front. Above all, perhaps, the generals were not looking for anything of this sort. They had persuaded themselves that the war was all but over. Their senses were deadened to any fresh perception (Hastings, p. 137).

For an on the ground report by an enlisted American soldier, consider a remembrance by then Sgt. Charles Rangel, later a long serving, black congressman from Harlem, New York, who was on the scene.

> Though we knew they were up there, during the day, we never saw the Chinese in the hills above us ... The tension rose to a crescendo with the eerie bugle blare. Then they hit. The Chinese poured over that Kunu-ri mountain pass just like ants swarming, from both sides of the road, screaming and yelling and bugling for all they were worth. We were stuck in defensive positions by a long line of trucks just trying to get the hell out of that situation. We were led by a Major John Fralish, who was acting as CO after any number of other officers were wounded, killed, or otherwise missing ... But plans for an orderly retreat fell apart as quickly as they were made, given the tremendous casualties, spotty communications, and repeated breaks in the chain of command between various units. Somehow Major Fralish kept us moving, by fits and starts, down the road toward Sunchon. But the Chinese troops were well positioned on both sides of the road, as it wound through increasingly higher hills approaching a narrow pass in the mountains between us and Sunchon. They were really playing cat and mouse with us, letting us get a little farther, then cutting off one part or another of our ragtag column (Rangel, p. 65).

Charlie Rangel managed to get himself and others with him south of the Chinese attackers.

> When we got over [the other side of a mountain]

there was a field hospital and medics waiting for us. They put me on a cart and there was a general congratulating me for leading the men through enemy lines. But in my first moment as a war hero I felt nothing but the shock of fleeing for my life, and the awe that I still had life. And because I appeared to be less scared than the forty-three enlisted men who followed me, I received the Bronze Star with the "V" device for valor (Rangel, pp. 68-69).

Parenthetically let me note that Rangel's recognition for valor helped him win election to the US House of Representatives in 1970 and in the elections thereafter until his retirement in 2017.

The details about the retreat, some called it the Big Bugout, of the Allied forces from North Korea can be omitted, but the overextended American and ROK troops made a costly and disorderly retreat back to South Korea. Losses of men were not huge and despite retreating, their firepower, including coverage by the American Air Force, imposed heavy casualties on the Chinese "volunteers." Still, note-worthy costs were incurred for captured and destroyed weaponry. As Halberstam says, near Pyongyang, the fleeing allies "passed huge bonfires visible from miles away, as vast stores of equipment, supplies that had still been coming into the country when the great offensive started, were destroyed, lest the gear be captured by the Chinese" (Halberstam, p. 483). The situation was similar in the east. At the port of Hamnung, one hundred thousand Allied troops were safely taken from the mainland by ship to be reorganized and resupplied at Pusan in the south.

Behind them an orgy of looting and destruction was taking place, as one of the greatest supply dumps in Korea was stripped by civilians or blown up by engineers. Pillars of black smoke plumed along the horizon behind the waterfront ... On December 24, with the evacuation completed, the U.S. Navy unleashed a huge bombardment on the abandoned port, blasting its facilities and remaining dumps into wreckage. It was much more a gesture of frustration, of embittered anger and disappointment, than of military utility (Hastings p. 164).

With hindsight and objectivity it is easy to suggest that after the success at Inchon, had McArthur held the line at or near the 38th parallel, the likelihood for an easier and less painful birth of a pair of Korean nations might have grown and prospered into mutual acceptance.

The chaotic retreat of UN forces in Korea brought confusion and contrary opinions in Washington about how to prosecute the war. At one extreme, the disconcerted McArthur, unable to accept blame for failure, now demanded more divisions and wanted enlarged authority to attack the Chinese on the mainland, even introducing nuclear weapons into the fight. At the opposite extreme were those who would withdraw from the fight entirely, ignoring friends and foes for self-preservation. Joseph P. Kennedy, father of John F. Kennedy, was a former American ambassador to Great Britain. Kennedy argued that America's flawed foreign policy required correction by withdrawal "from Korea, Berlin and the defense of Western Europe" (Acheson, p. 488). There were fears that the poor American military results in Korea would embolden the Soviets in Europe and other parts of the world. Republicans in the Senate were wary about introducing American ground forces in Europe to strengthen the NATO alliance. There were differing efforts in the UN to call for a ceasefire. The Chinese called for a ceasefire, the withdrawal of the US from both Korea and Formosa, and demanded its own seat in the UN. The Truman administration settled on a policy of standing firm in Korea. It would stabilize the military situation on the peninsula as close to 38th parallel as feasible and fight a limited war, intending keep casualties to a minimum while imposing as much damage and punishment on the Chinese and North Korean forces as possible.

The limited war policy was firmed up by a circumstantial

forward step when General Walton Walker died in a Jeep accident in late December. In his stead, General Matthew Ridgway was put in command of the US Eighth Army. Within a matter of months, Ridgway's leadership on the battlefield brought remarkable changes in strategy, tactical details, field commanders, shortened supply lines, and careful choices about the grounds for battle. He was credited for taking a defeated force and turning it around.

> From the outset, Ridgway demanded a new attention to terrain, and the assessment of key features that must be defended. There would be a fresh focus upon defense – and attack – in depth, with unit flanks secured against infiltration. Above all, the Army must get off the roads, must be willing to reach for and hold high ground ... He had no patience with the preoccupation among the Eighth Army... with evacuation of the peninsula. Ridgway did not believe this should be remotely necessary. The only contingency for which he was willing to prepare was withdrawal to a new Pusan Perimeter – but this one would be dug and prepared on an unprecedented scale (Hastings p. 190).

Flushed with their recent success, the Chinese were intent upon forcing the UN troops out of Korea entirely. At Mao's direction, the Chinese and North Korean forces successfully pushed south of the 38th parallel. They recaptured Seoul. On February 11, 1951, they began what they designated as a "fourth offensive" against the US and ROK positions. In a bitter series of battles, their success was limited and their advance ground to a halt within a week. The tide of battle turned, with the UN forces recapturing the devastated Seoul in mid-March. By the end of March, the Allies again crossed north of the 38th parallel. "But this time there was to be no headlong race for the Yalu. Ridgway's objective was merely to reach the 'Iron Triangle' south of Pyongyang, the heart of the Communist supply and communications network" (Hastings, pp. 197-198).

After that, there were seesaw movements, surge and fall

back battle movements. "It became a war of cruel, costly battles, of few breakthroughs, and of strategies designed to inflict maximum punishment on the other side without essentially changing the battle lines. In the end, there would be no great victory for anyone, only some kind of mutually unsatisfactory compromise" (Halberstam p. 624). The Allies had better artillery, air support, and technology for command and control. The North Koreans and Chinese had more men and were willing to expend them in human wave attacks, only to be met by overwhelming firepower and a huge cost in casualties. It was a war of attrition rather than dramatic victories or defeats.

The reversal of fortunes suffered by the UN forces in North Korea reflected hugely and negatively upon MacArthur because he had forecast no entry by the Chinese into the hostilities and that the conflict would be over by Thanksgiving, allowing American troops to be pulling out by Christmas. The entry into the conflict by the Chinese turned those blue sky forecasts into a bitter winter of combat. After he became alarmed, MacArthur wanted more troops, more resources, and even a wider war, possibly using atomic weapons. When his requests were denied by the Truman administration, which had settled on a limited war strategy, MacArthur brashly went to the press, publicly calling for a larger war. He wanted the right to bomb the Chinese north of the Yalu border. On December 6, 1950, an angry President Truman ordered military commanders to cease direct contacts with the press about "military or foreign policy," a restriction aimed particularly at MacArthur (Acheson, p. 472). In the following months, MacArthur continued to bicker with the Joint Chiefs about the next steps. Meanwhile, at the operational level, General Ridgway was succeeding at stabilizing his forces near the 38th parallel and imposing heavy casualties upon the Chinese. But MacArthur persisted in demanding a clean sweep of North Korea, insisting that his mission was to gain a full unification of the entire peninsula as one nation. President Truman and his administration made it abundantly clear that the mission was to take and hold a defensible line near the middle of the peninsula and that a long-term solution would be settled by negotiations and United Nations' oversight after that. By the middle of March 1951, the president was preparing a ceasefire proposal to begin a diplomatic process aimed to gain a long-term peace agreement. Informed of this, MacArthur burst forth in public from Japan with his own provocative statement on March 24, threatening the Chinese mainland and calling for direct negotiations between himself as military commander and the "commander in chief of the enemy forces" to realize the "political objectives of the United Nations in Korea ... without further bloodshed" (Acheson, p. 756). Such an unjustified presumption of power and authority was way beyond the bounds of MacArthur's assigned military responsibility. He rashly intruded upon the constitutionally-elected president's war powers and the administration's authority for international negotiations.

President Truman's hammer did not fall on MacArthur immediately. In March, MacArthur was in touch with the Republican minority leader of the House of Representatives, Joe Martin, calling for the use of presidentially forbidden troops, the Nationalist Chinese, and calling for total victory in all of Korea. Martin made MacArthur's letter public in the House, making obvious MacArthur's willingness to politically challenge the policy judgments of the president and the administration MacArthur was sworn to serve. President Truman took counsel with his top advisers and concluded that MacArthur had to be fired. Truman intended to do it with courtesy, but under pressure because of likely news leaks, it was officially announced at a late news conference on April 11, 1951. MacArthur actually received the first word about it from his wife, who received the news secondhand from a radio news report (Jager, p. 177). With MacArthur out of the way, Matthew Ridgway was promoted to overall command in Asia and General James Van Fleet assumed Ridgway's assignment in Korea.

President Truman and his administration received heavy

criticism over the MacArthur firing. Upon departing Japan, MacArthur was praised by the Japanese for the generous post-war occupation he oversaw there. In New York, there was a huge ticker-tape parade honoring him for his previous heroics. A joint session of Congress heard an emotionally appealing speech from MacArthur. He continued his argument against his superiors by saying, "The tragedy of Korea is further heightened by the fact that its military action is confined to its territorial limits" (The speech is available at www.presentationmagazine.com/general-macarthur-speech-7523.html). But those were his orders, limits he wanted not to accept. There were many emotional responses from MacArthur's supporters who produced telegrams protesting the president's action. At the White House, the early count was "three to one against his removal" (Jager, p. 179). But the storm of public opinion abated and many military experts and editorial opinions argued for the wisdom and prudence of Truman's decision. "After Senate hearings investigating MacArthur's dismissal had shown that Truman's decision to relieve the general had been unanimously backed by Secretary of Defense Marshall and the JCS, public opinion turned in favor of the president" (Jager, p. 180).

For a helpful judgment on this issue, Max Hastings, a British authority on matters of military history, provides a well-studied assessment thirty-five years after the Korean conflict wound down:

> It was Truman's misfortune that MacArthur chanced to be commanding in Tokyo when the Korean conflict began. The accident was compounded by the hesitancy and weakness with which Washington handled this Olympian figure through the months that followed. Inchon was indeed a master stroke, but it was a perverse tragedy for MacArthur and those around him because its success prevented them from confronting the fact that his judgment was gone. He was too remote, too old, too inflexible, too deeply imprisoned by a world vision that

was obsolete to be a fit commander in such a war as Korea. It was fortunate that his removal was eventually achieved before he could inflict an historic military, moral, or political disaster upon the West's cause in Asia (Hastings, p. 207).

The United States increased the tempo of the war by increasing its use of air power. Dubbed Operation Strangle, the Allies conducted over a million air sorties during the conflict, most described as "close cover" (Hastings, p. 266). To some surprise, the Russian MiG-15s had an early successful kill-to-loss ratio over the Americans in their F-80s (Wada, p. 202). However, introducing the F-86 Sabres obtained "almost undisputed dominance in the skies over Korea, North and South" (Hastings, p. 259). The Allies bombed the road system and the railways, seeking to interdict communist supplies coming from China and the USSR. " 'Strangle' cost the UN air forces 343 aircraft destroyed and 290 damaged, mostly fighter-bombers. It proved to objective observers, such as Ridgway, that there was 'simply no such thing as choking off supply lines in a country is wild as North Korea' " (Hastings, p. 267). With control of the skies, the UN forces continued to bomb the North to the point that US Air Force Chief of Staff General Hoyt Vandenberg complained, "We have reached the point where there are not enough targets left in North Korea to keep the air force busy" (Jager, p. 257). As the bombing did continue, the Chinese response was to tunnel underground. "By August 1952 the Chinese had dug 125 miles of tunnels and 400 miles of trenches. By the end of the war the Chinese had built an astonishing 780 miles of tunnels that formed underground cities" (Jager, pp. 240-241). The tunnels were to protect the North's forces from devastating air attacks.

By the summer of 1951, there was evidence of willingness by both sides to enter into negotiations – not really for peace, but for some sort of ceasefire agreement. However, the fact of negotiations did not end the fighting. The military ebb and flow continued on both sides while negotiators were exchanging views. As Wada has reported, the primary decision makers consulting together and calling the shots on the communist side were Stalin and the USSR, along with Mao and China. At the bargaining table it was the Chinese who were the visible negotiators, not the Russians. On many specific details, "the Chinese delegation did not consult their North Korean colleagues" (Wada, p. 190). In the meantime, South Korea's Rhee and North Korea's Kim each harbored hopes that his side would prevail in gaining control of the entire peninsula.

Progress on the negotiating front came in October 1951. According to Wada, Mao could see advantage in a ceasefire. Mao's correspondence with Stalin records: "Peace through the armistice talks would be advantageous for us, however, we do not fear a delay in negotiations. Proceeding this way, we will certainly gain victory. At the same time, domestically we will carry out successfully various measures and in the political and economic spheres we can attain stability and greater development" (Wada, p. 204). With that assumption in place, the Chinese proposed a truce line north of the 38th parallel, "provided the UN agreed to its implementation immediately. In effect, they proposed that the fighting stop before the other issues are resolved and an armistice is put into effect" (Jager, p. 200). Although Ridgway was suspicious of delay, in Washington there was impatience to get some agreement leading to a resolution for this unpopular war. "The truce-line agreement was finalized on November 27 over Ridgway's strong objections" (Jager, p. 201). Then, for thirty days, no progress was made in the talks. "By December 27, when it was amply apparent at Panmunjom that the Communist delegation had merely been playing for time, their armies were dug into the positions that, with only a few minor variations, would form the final armistice line nineteen months later" (Hastings, p. 233).

Although the DPRK and the ROK had representation in the negotiations, the Soviets and the Chinese on one side, and the US, representing the UN, on the other, were the primary decision makers. The first issue was where precisely would the dividing line be? UN forces were willing to accept a twelve-mile wide demilitarized zone, but wanted it north of the 38th parallel. The communists quit the talks, and in the next two months the UN command moved the battle line north about fifteen miles.

Talks picked up again in November, but the UN Command was on to another issue, objecting to an all-for-all prisoner exchange. There were vastly more prisoners of war (POWs) in the South than in the North. Moreover, many of the captives held by the UN did not want to be repatriated. The UN conducted a screening process said to have been "actually designed to favor repatriation," but "the screening revealed that of about 132,000 of its POWs, only 70,000 wanted to be returned. The UN was willing to exchange the 70,000 for about 12,000 POWs held by the North. The Communists refused and talks collapsed in April 1952" (Jager, pp. 206-207). In the meantime, the conflict in the hills of Korea moved one way and then another. "By May 1952, the war seemed to have reached a moral and physical stalemate. It would take a new American president to move the struggle forward, even at the risk of a nuclear war" (Jager, p. 265).

Peace negotiations at Panmunjom were going nowhere. In October 1952, the US went to the UN to push for an armistice that called for the Chinese and North Koreans to "agree to an armistice which recognizes the rights of all prisoners of war to an unrestricted opportunity to be repatriated and avoids the use of force in their repatriation" (Acheson, p. 609). Despite support in the UN for that principle, the communist side still rejected the proposition. By December 1952, the Truman administration, about to be turned over to the Republicans, and Acheson, soon to be retired, turned their attention to the details of a governmental transition.

Perhaps the political forces in the US partly explain the dragging arguments with the communists. The American political context had shifted. The Democrats had controlled the presidency since the 1932 election. In 1952, Truman's popularity was at a low standing. On March 29, Truman, although eligible for another term of the presidency, announced he would not run for reelection. In the Republican Party, there was a battle between Robert Taft and Republican conservatives against the more moderate wing of that party and its champion, Dwight D. Eisenhower. At its July convention, the Republicans chose Eisenhower as their presidential nominee. He would face Adlai Stevenson, who was nominated by the Democrats. The issue of peace in Korea was of headline significance during the campaign. On October 24, 1952, "Eisenhower delivered his speech ... on the sharpest issue of the campaign, pledging that if elected, 'I shall go to Korea,' and declaring it was his 'goal' to end the war there" (Lyon, p. 463). As a scholarly study of the 1952 election would later reveal,

> In 1952 the public unquestionably was searching for a solution to an irregular war that had become oppressive, and its vote appears to have been in large part an expression of lack of confidence in the capacity of the Democratic Party to deal with the problem ... It is very doubtful indeed if the voters who elected Mr. Eisenhower to the presidency had any clear idea of exactly what he and the Republican Party proposed to do about the Korean War, except that Eisenhower would make a personal inspection. Their mandate to the president-elect was to produce a solution and far from prescribing specific policies he should follow, they gave him virtually unlimited freedom of action (Campbell et al., *The American Voter*, p. 546).

After the election but before his inauguration, Eisenhower made a then secret trip to Korea, spending three days in consultation, mostly with his former military colleagues, Generals Mark Clark and James Van Fleet; along with getting near the front, he inspected some troops, visited an army hospital, and even spent an hour with Syngman Rhee (Hastings, p. 317). Eisenhower headed home, apparently convinced not to widen the war but to gain a truce.

Mao expected the worst after Eisenhower took office, that

"he would launch an offensive in Korea to break the stale-mate in the war" (Wada, p. 251). Mao expressed those concerns to Stalin and asked for more Russian weapons. But Stalin apparently wanted an end to the conflict and even responded to a *New York Times* initiated series of questions. For a front-page article by James Reston on Christmas day, Stalin responded to a question about coop-eration with a "diplomatic approach designed to bring about an end to the Korean War." The answer he gave was, "I agree to cooperate because the U.S.S.R. is interested in ending the war in Korea." Reston went on to speculate that "whether the Premier's expressed willingness to consider a new diplomatic approach to ending the Korean war will be fruitful, will depend upon the reception given to the reply by the new [Eisenhower] Administration" (*New York Times*, December 25, 1952).

The Eisenhower administration did some saber rattling in the spring of 1953. In January, the US successfully tested an atomic device that could be adapted for delivery by artil-lery. The new secretary of state, John Foster Dulles, let it be known that the US might bomb targets on the Chinese side of the China-North Korea border. However, there was movement on prisoner exchange. The International Red Cross had suggested an exchange of sick and wounded prisoners as a first step toward an exchange process. Called "Operation Little Switch," General Clark took up the suggestion in February 1953. In the first week of March, Stalin died from a "sudden brain hemorrhage" (Jager, p. 273). The Soviets promptly became conciliatory. So did President Eisenhower. In a speech entitled "The Chance for Peace," he called for an honorable armistice in Korea. Operation Little Switch was agreed to and implemented between April 30 and May 3 when 5,800 POWs were sent North and 600 were returned South. The exchange was completed at Panmunjom.

In June, most of the terms for an armistice were set. Totally unsatisfied with a truce that called for a divided peninsula, Syngman Rhee took a provocative action of his own. He set free 27,000 anti-communist North Korean POWs intending to throw a wrench into the negotiations. Despite that back-stabbing effort, the Americans and the Chinese wanted a settlement and proceeded with it anyway. It was signed Panmunjom on July 27, 1953, and each side imposed a ceasefire at ten o'clock that evening. There followed quite promptly another prisoner exchange. Hastings describes the details of the settlement.

> Within a month of the commencement of 'Operation Big Switch' on August 5, 75,823 Communist prisoners had been sent north, 5,640 of these Chinese. The Communists, in their turn, handed over 12,773 men, 3,597 of them American, 7,862 South Korea. The Neutral Nations Repatriation Commission in the demilitarized zone took over 22,604 prisoners from the United Nations. Of these, 137 eventually agreed to repatriation. The remainder elected for resettlement South Korea or Formosa. Of the prisoners in Communist hands, 359 initially declined to go home. Ten of these – two American and eight Korean – changed their minds while in the custody of the Repatriation Commission. But for the remainder – 325 Koreans, 21 Americans and one Briton (Andrew Condron) – there was no emotional arrival at Freedom Village. To the astonishment and profound dismay of their countrymen, they chose to join the society of their former captors (Hastings, p. 328).

Neither side "won the war," but the UN allies on one side and the communist regimes of China and the Soviet Union all wished to wash their hands of the conflict. *Izvestia*, the Soviet newspaper that reported the communist party line, congratulated its leaders for the truce under the title, "The Great Victory of the Camp of Peace and Democracy." It said that the armistice was "a major contribution to peace" and that it "inspired trust." As Wada notes, "Stalin's succes-sors thus sang the praises of their successful diplomacy" (Wada, p. 284). If the mood of the American people was apathy and relief, President Eisenhower considered the armistice a significant achievement. "He had promised to go to Korea and end the killing and he did" (Jager, p. 285). What was unresolved was the next steps by the peninsula's leaders on both sides of the truce line. Given their bitter enmity, neither Kim Il Sung nor Syngman Rhee wanted to live with a two-Korea solution for the Korean people. Peace negotiations were conducted by international tribunals in Panmunjom and later, during 1954, in Geneva. The two Koreas were still at odds, whether their allies agreed or not. The conflict ended with no treaty of peace because there really was no positive agreement. After alternating but unaccepted proposals had been exchanged, a spokesman for the UN forces declared that there was no purpose for further negotiations.

Peace talks on the Korean question were now over and the armistice system became permanent. The war had started because unification could not be achieved peacefully, but use of military force had failed, and diplomacy had achieved nothing at the conference table. As a result, huge armies faced each other uneasily across the military demarcation line just as they had when the cease-fire started in 1953. Divided into two hostile states, the Korean Peninsula was neither at peace nor at war (Wada, p. 291).

CHAPTER 3: HOME GROWN LEADERSHIP IN NORTH AND SOUTH KOREA

Previous reference has been made to two major players in the drama of a divided Korea: Syngman Rhee in the Republic of Korea, and Kim Il Sung in the Democratic People's Republic of Korea. The hastily agreed upon plan to divide the Korean Peninsula for initial administration by the Soviet Union and the United States was established by the major powers before the end of World War II without any input from Korean leaders. Implementation occurred in 1945 by the introduction of military forces: the Soviet Union occupying the north and the United States in the south. There was only a vague understanding between the Soviets and the United States that a trusteeship would be established until a single Korean government could be put into place for the entire Korean Peninsula. Relatively soon, however, there were Korean aspirants for leadership both in the Soviet-controlled North and the US-administered South.

In 1945, when the US Army took administrative control of South Korea, the task was difficult and chaotic. Initially the responsibility was imposed by MacArthur on General John R. Hodge. With little preparation for the job and no explicit appreciation for Korea, Koreans, or their culture, Hodge tried to operate the society by retaining the former Japanese occupiers in key administrative positions. That practice severely offended the Koreans. Koreans were anxious for relief from the constraints imposed by their former Japanese oppressors. The Japanese got the message. Relatively promptly, tens of thousands of Japanese left South Korea for their Japanese homeland. Meanwhile, Koreans from Manchuria and the Soviet-dominated North were streaming into the South and bringing along a vision for a communistic society. Dealing with the distressed population under his authority, General Hodge needed to identify Korean leaders sympathetic to American interests in order to establish an effective capitalistic- and democratically-oriented administration. Imagine Hodge's sense of relief to find help from an American-educated Korean who loved his countrymen, favored capitalism, revealed leadership ability, and spoke intelligent English. Into a vacuum of leadership in South Korea, Syngman Rhee made an entrance. Jager introduces Rhee this way:

> Someone without links to the colonial regime, but with nationalist standing among the Koreans, was needed. KDP [Korean Democratic Party] leaders suggested Syngman Rhee (Yi Sung-man, [his original Korean name]). In many ways, Rhee was the perfect candidate. He had spent much of his life overseas, mostly in the United States, where he earned a PhD from Princeton in 1910. After a two-year stint in Seoul as a Christian educator and missionary, he returned to the States in 1912. In 1919 he was elected the first president of the Korean Provisional Government (KPG), a government in exile in Shanghai. He went back to the United States in 1925 after being expelled by the KPG and remained there until the end of World War II. While in the States, he was politically active in the Korean independence movement. He was fluent in English as well as untainted by association with the [Japanese] colonial regime. Rhee was 70 years old in 1945, but vigorous. He was also difficult, stubborn, and fiercely patriotic ... Rhee's stint as president of the KPG was marked by strife.

He tried hard to get American recognition of the KPG as the legitimate government of Korea during the colonial period. Some in the State Department found him and other KPG leaders 'personally ambitious and somewhat irresponsible' and down-played the clout of the KPG 'even among exiles.' Nevertheless, Hodge and his advisors were eager to embrace him, believing that the legitimacy Rhee could bring to the KDP and the promise of Korean independence might be enough to stem the tide of political chaos in their zone (Jager, pp.37-38).

The Americans were stuck with a commitment to the earlier idea for a provisional government that would administer the entire Korean Peninsula under the Soviet Union, China, Britain, and the United States. That vision, of course, was never successful. The failed peace begat a bloody war that ended in an awkward stalemate. The Soviet Union had the North as its client nation. The US struggled along with a military administration that tried to work with an emerging democratic, but anti-communist, local leadership. As the reality of an Iron Curtain separating the Soviet Union and its eastern European communist governments from the NATO countries dominated by the US, the notion of a long-term separation between North and South Korea crystallized. As noted previously, the Republic of Korea (ROK) was declared on August 15, 1948. At that time, Syngman Rhee was chosen as President by the National Assembly.

Rhee's distinguishing characteristic was that he opposed the communists totally. His commitment to democracy was only to the measure that he could retain support from a South Korean majority. But Rhee was by no means a protector of individual rights and freedom of expression. A dark stain on the Rhee administration followed the entry of the Chinese volunteers into the war on the North's side in late 1950. As the UN forces fell back, units of the South Korean government conducted mass executions of political opponents during December. "The daily executions after the fall of Pyongyang became too egregious to ignore ... [E]ight hundred persons described as convicted Communists, collaborators, saboteurs, and murderers were executed during the second week of December alone" (Jager, p. 148). There were numerous incidents of that sort. The British allies became so incensed that one of the British brigade commanders "ordered his men to shoot any South Korean policemen attempting to carry out executions ... near his troops' encampment ... Eventually, Rhee, who had initially ordered the executions speeded up, backed down and, conceding to international pressure, suspended mass executions" (Jager, pp. 149-150). The viciousness of Korean-on-Korean retribution was evidenced on both sides, but it greatly undermined the morale among South Korea's United Nations' supporters and motivated distrust for Rhee and his administration.

During 1952, while the war raged on, Rhee was in a tumultuous political conflict with members of the ROK National Assembly. Rhee wanted a constitutional amendment to provide for direct election of the president. Resistance to Rhee in the National Assembly provoked Rhee to declare martial law and arrest some of the Assembly members. Responding to challenges from Americans, Rhee charged that his opponents were part of an alleged communist plot. Eventually, President Truman called upon Rhee to protect, not attack, the principles of constitutional government. At the time there were discussions in Washington about whether or not to remove Rhee from the ROK presidency by force. That plan was not implemented. Eventually, in July, Rhee got his way when the National Assembly adopted a constitutional amendment that provided for direct election of a president and a bicameral legislature. In the subsequent election in August, Rhee won the presidency with over five million out of seven million votes cast. "Rhee, his power base strengthened ... emerged from South Korea's crisis stronger than ever, though Rhee now went along with Washington's wishes" (Wada, p. 234).

Rhee's unreliability regarding American wishes became obvious during the armistice negotiations. The exchange of prisoners was a thorny issue. Rhee wanted the UN to take a hard line regarding the war, to fight the DPRK until a single nation unification could be effected. But when negotiations at Panmunjom neared a resolution for two distinct nations, Rhee did his best to undermine the agreement. "Rhee surreptitiously ordered the ROK Army to release twenty-seven thousand anti-Communist North Korean prisoners held in its custody ... The release of the prisoners had been carefully planned. The idea originated with Rhee himself" (Jager, p. 279). Although Rhee had the support of the South Korean people for this action, it was a behind-the-back effort to disrupt the peace negotiations. There was outrage expressed in Washington and by Washington's international allies. Nevertheless, because the communists wanted out of this conflict as much as the UN allies did, the armistice was agreed to and signed on July 27, 1953. Neither Rhee nor Kim Il Sung could stand in the way of the armistice settlement.

Even after the armistice was put in place, with the ROK's independence backed by American military assurances, Rhee continued to be a prickly ally to the United States. Rhee wanted to be a visible force in the Asian region, but to achieve it, he tried to manipulate American military strength. In May 1954, Rhee was agitating for the United States to sponsor a huge standing military force under its Far Eastern Command to meet the challenge of expanding communist power, "or we shall run the terrible risk of losing Thailand, Malaysia, Burma, Indonesia and other countries to the enemy ... Large numbers of communist advisers are serving the Indo-Chinese rebels and there are well authenticated reports that at least some Red forces have been employed in belligerent actions." Pushing the idea of a Red Menace in Asia, Rhee went on to offer two divisions of his army for the purpose. "Let the United States provide armaments and the other nations of Asia will provide the men" (Rhee, *New York Times*, May 9, 1954). Convinced of a domino theory of communist aggression, and with limited resources of his own, Rhee wanted to rattle the American sword in Asia against his imagined Armageddon. A sage and appropriately skeptical Eisenhower administration refused to be moved by Rhee's anti-communist passions.

Rhee presided over a domestic list of economic and social adversities. He preserved the form of democracy but his style was authoritarian. During his presidency, he was remarkably successful at soliciting American assistance.

Although Rhee had leveraged South Korea's strategic position in the cold war to wheedle hundreds of millions of dollars in military and economic aid from the United States, he had little to show for his efforts, as much of the aid was siphoned off to line the pockets of corrupt officials. Nearly a decade after the war, the country, with its tiny domestic market and thoroughly aggrieved population, still lacked resources of domestic capital (Jager, pp. 337-338).

Unemployment and a weak economy led to poverty, corruption, and despair in the ROK despite the fact that it was a beneficiary of huge amounts of American aid.

In response to widespread attempts by Rhee's political allies to rig the election outcome in March 1960, street riots by students turned to public revulsion for the Rhee administration. After weeks of chaos, the US sternly rebuked the Koreans with messages from Secretary of State Christian Herter and the US ambassador to Korea. Calling for a preservation of fair elections, Secretary Herter acknowledged the corruption of the election process which would have justified the reelection of eighty-five-year-old president Rhee and a hand-picked successor (William J. Jordan, *New York Times*, April 20, 1960). Under US pressure, Rhee publicly resigned and a caretaker government was formed, making way for new elections ("Arc of Crisis," *New York Times*, May 1, 1960). The US softened the personal cost for Rhee himself, allowing him a comfortable retirement to Hawaii. Eventually, the ROK would develop an effective democracy after a stint of governance through the military.

Kim Il Sung's fortune in Pyongyang was much different.

Geopolitics also operated to Kim's advantage. The emerging split within the Communist bloc between the Chinese and the Soviets benefited the North Korean regime handsomely as both capitals vied for the allegiance of the North. Thus, rather than being rejected by Stalin or Mao for his failed war, Kim was courted by both sides in the years following the war, as Stalin and Mao wanted to legitimate their dominance in the movement by having smaller Communist countries, like the DPRK, on their side.

During Stalin's life, Mao willingly deferred to the Soviet leadership of the communist movement. But after Stalin's death in 1953, Mao and the Chinese increasingly differed with Nikita Khrushchev, the new Soviet leader. "Mao was becoming increasingly critical of Khrushchev's principle of 'peaceful coexistence' between the socialist and nonsocialist worlds. He accused Khrushchev of abandoning the class struggle" (Jager, p. 313). As the two monoliths of the communist world developed contrasting strategies about international domination, Kim "learned to play off his communist sponsors against each other to his own advantage" (Oberdorfer and Carlin, p. 9). Kim managed to get both communist mega-powers to make treaty agreements promising the DPRK cooperation and mutual assistance.

The war and its aftermath left devastating effects on both sides of the armistice line. Both capital cities, Seoul and Pyongyang, were physically decimated. If the total of the war's fatalities remain undetermined, the estimated combat deaths are between three and four million persons (Wada, p. 293). The war brought differences in the North and South Korean populations. The heavy bombing by the US that forced North Koreans underground led to severe infections of tuberculosis that demobilized as many as a quarter of a million DPRK soldiers (Jager, p. 357). The active communists in the South mostly escaped or moved to the North. Correspondingly, most of the Christians in the North fled to the South. Extended families that were spread across the peninsula were separated by the arbitrary armistice line. On both sides of the line, the political leadership, unsatisfied with the armistice, emphasized a distinctive brand of nationalism. The North would heavily impose a brand of state socialism modeled after the Soviet Union. The South, committed to free enterprise, had to endure a weak and struggling economy with little capitalization of industry along with a wobbly and corrupt democracy.

North Korea, despite the devastation of war, had remnants of heavy industry, a well-developed electrical power grid, and well-known mineral deposits.

> Only two weeks after the August 1953 armistice ending the war, Kim Il Sung gave a speech titled 'Everything for the Postwar Rehabilitation and Development for the People.' The first Three-Year Plan's (1954-1956) focus was on reconstruction and expansion of heavy industry as the basis of national power. Kim Il Sung received heavy industrial equipment, power plants, hydroelectric dams, electrified railroads, and irrigation systems from Soviet benefactors. China offered crude oil, food, and fertilizer. North Korea gained additional currency by exporting gold, zinc, steel, and minerals to both Moscow and Beijing (Cha, p. 23).

The Soviets helped with the mechanization of agriculture and chemical fertilization for the North's crops. As a result, the people of the North were better fed than those in the South from the 1950s throughout most of the 1970s. The political beneficiary of this success was Kim Il Sung. During the late 1950s, he was able to eliminate rivals for leadership. As he did so, the language of public policy increasingly emphasized Korean self-determination and steered a course different from the socialism of the Soviet Union. Stalin and Stalinism was gone from the Soviet Union. The new Stalin of the DPRK, however, was clearly Kim Il Sung. For the people, he articulated an ideology of ethnic identity and nationalism expressed as *juche*.

Under *juche*, North Korea could not rely on the good graces of others, it had to fend for its self and preserve true Korean identity. In an ideological context, *juche* consisted of four formal tenets: (1) man is the master of his fate; (2) the master of the Revolution is the people; (3) the Revolution must be pursued in a self-reliant manner; and (4) the key to Revolution is loyalty to the supreme leader, or *Suryong*, Kim Il Sung. It was communist in that it constituted a partial adoption of Marxism and Leninism. It accepted, for example, that capitalists and imperialists were the enemy and that the Revolution would be won in a class struggle by laborers over their oppressors ... [I]t stressed the role of man's efforts as the primary mover of history (Cha, pp. 37-38).

This unique revision of communism was stretched and altered over time until the concept of *Suryong* (leader) was personified. "At the Fifth Party Congress in 1970, *juche* was formally adopted as the sole guiding principle of the state. It evolved over time, largely through the work of Kim Jong Il, from a political ideology to a cult of personality in which Kim Il Sung came to have godlike qualities as the embodiment and savior of the Korean race" (Cha, pp. 38-39). Drawing upon Koreans' understanding of Confucian thought, Kim sought to assume in his person the parental role in relation to "his" Korean people. The people would express filial piety in their respect for Kim, the father of the country. The father-leader owed his people the benefits of their collective efforts to serve the state.

Elaborating the theory provided a rationale for continuing contention against South Korea. That rival state in the South functioned under American hegemony and allowed a large US military contingent to defend the armistice border at the 38th parallel. By contrast, the Soviets and Chinese withdrew from the DPRK. The DPRK could blame the American intruders for standing in the way of unification. Thus the DPRK considered itself justified in appealing to

Koreans in the South to instigate revolution and use whatever means available to unite all the people of the Korean Peninsula under the DPRK flag. For an outsider's perspective on Kim's success in building the *juche* ideology into solid popular support for himself and his regime, consider a leading American journalistic account.

For a visitor from afar, the most extraordinary thing about the Kim Il Sung era was the unrestrained adoration, bordering on idolatry, built up around the Great Leader, which seemed to reflect a craving for adulation that could never be sated. Kim's photograph, later joined by a separate picture of his son Kim Jong Il, was on the wall in every home as well as every shop and office. Starting in the 1960s, at the son's order, every North Korean adult wore a badge bearing the senior Kim's likeness on his or her suit, tunic, or dress.

Within his country Kim was nearly always referred to as *suryong*, or Great Leader, a term referring to the greatest of the great that Kim reserved for Lenin, Stalin, and Mao before he began applying it to himself in the 1960s ...

Kim created an impermeable and absolutist state that many have compared to a religious cult. No dissent from or criticism of Kim Il Sung, his tenets, or his decisions was permitted. Citizens were arrested, and some even sent off to one of the country's extensive gulags, for inadvertently defacing or sitting on a newspaper photograph of the Great Leader or his son and chosen successor. Reports of inhumane treatment, torture and public execution for failure to conform to all forms of adoration for the Kims were rife. Prison camps were established in remote areas containing as many as 150,000 people, many of whom were held in ghastly, inhumane conditions with little chance of ever being released (Oberdorfer and Carlin, pp. 16-17).

This inhumane Kim, as he is known in the rest of the world, is not the one known by his people. The Kim they know led a guerrilla army that defeated the Japanese and expelled the outsiders from the North. Thus he has taken up his rightful and exalted role as leader of his people.

> Every North Korean child today believes that the Korean War was started by South Korea and the United States in a surprise attack on June 25, 1950. They believe that Kim Il Sung repelled the Americans and within three days, drove U.S. forces south to the Pusan perimeter. There is no mention of the Chinese intervention in the war, nor that the instigator of the war was Kim himself. Kim Il Sung has since been recorded in North Korean history as the ultimate leader, the epitome of everything Korean, and everything good in the world. Though he passed away July 1994, the government designates him as the Eternal President of the country, forever alive in the spirit of North Koreans, even as his body lies in state in the Kim Il Sung Mausoleum on the outskirts of Pyongyang (Cha, p. 66).

After the student riots in South Korea that ousted Syngman Rhee and his corrupt cohorts from governmental control, John M. Chang, a teacher turned politician, was made premier. Although credited in the American press as one who addressed and reduced the governmental corruption of the past, the country was still floundering economically despite Chang's efforts at reform. "Foreigners here say that the Chang Government is not wildly popular because it has had to carry the economic burden of partition of the country and they had heritages of war and maladministration" (Rosenthal, *New York Times*, March 15, 1961). If Chang was not a dynamic leader, his opposition seemed to have no answers to the country's problems either. It was in that wobbly condition that Park Chung Hee made a military move.

While the civil and economic institutions of the Republic of Korea were weak, the ROK Army was a highly organized force. Army and marine troops led by General Park Chung Hee took over the government in a bloodless coup against the inept, previous regime. With the military's firm support, Park could exercise real power. Despite early concern for democracy in South Korea, Park's steady hand gained American friends as a counterforce opposing communism in Asia. Then, provided with substantial American technological assistance and Japanese capital, Park focused upon the economic development of his country.

Park Chung Hee's career before the presidency of South Korea differed substantially from his predecessor, Syngman Rhee, as well as that of his North Korean rival, Kim Il Sung. Unlike Kim, big and gregarious, Park was a small, quiet man who came from humble beginnings, the son of a farmer from a small village near Taegu in the peninsula's southeast quarter. Born in 1917, he went to teachers' college, taught in an elementary school for a few years, and then joined the Japanese army. He received Japanese military academy training and became a junior officer in the Japanese Army in 1944. In Manchuria, he fought against guerrilla units comprised of Korean expatriates, opposite the forces with which Kim Il Sung fought. After the Japanese surrender, he returned to southern Korea and took a place in the Korean Constabulary, an armed force that eventually formed the ROK Army. During the civil chaos in Korea during the late 1940s, Park followed his older brother into the South Korean Workers' Party, where he was caught up in civil violence that led to his arrest and a death sentence. However, a mentor of his, who was a colonel in the ROK Army, helped him obtain a commuted sentence from President Rhee and eventually enter the ROK Army. There, after the DPRK invasion, his training and leadership skills were recognized and he was commissioned as a major. He gained steady promotions during the war and by the armistice in 1953, he was a one-star general. Intending to remain in the ROK Army, he received six months of training in the US from the American military. By 1960, he was chief of operations staff for the ROK Army. During the chaotic time following the resignation of Rhee, there were rumors about military reorganization. That triggered a military coup, described as "wildly popular" (Jager, p. 341), out of which Park emerged as the leader. A devotee of disciplined planning and an admirer of Japan's rapid industrialization after World War II, Park led more like a communist than a democratic capitalist.

Only a month after seizing power, Park established the Economic Planning Council, which later became the Economic Planning Board, to provide central governmental direction for the economy. The first five-year development plan, produced shortly thereafter, declared that 'the economic system will be a form of guided capitalism, in which the principle of free exercise enterprise and respect for freedom and initiative of free enterprise will be observed, but in which the government will either directly participate or indirectly render guidance to the basic industries and other important fields' (Oberdorfer and Carlin, p. 28).

Park capitalized upon the early progress and popularity of the new regime while responding to American concerns expressed by the Kennedy administration. Instead of holding a referendum in which the people likely would have extended military rule, a proposition opposed by Washington, the Park regime drafted a constitution that was approved by the people in December 1962 and agreed to future elections. Park received the presidential nomination of the Democratic Republican Party and won the election to the presidency by a majority vote in 1963. After electing Park as president and members of a new Assembly, two and a half years of military rule ended. On a rain-soaked day, a crowd that included prominent Americans (Generals Matthew Ridgway and James Van Fleet, along with President Lyndon Johnson's envoy, James Burns), Park took his oath of office. The Americans were there to express approval for Park's restoration of constitutional rule.

"Once ensconced" under a constitution that provided for

strong executive powers with a weak unicameral legislature, "Park skillfully used the powers of incumbency for building new networks of political support around the presidency" (Haggard, Kim and Moon, p. 856). He also "took personal charge of the economy, bringing highly professional economists, many of them American educated, into the planning agencies ... Park incessantly visited government offices in the economic area and construction sites in the field to check up on what was happening" (Oberdorfer and Carlin, p. 28).

In 1964, Park responded to an opportunity to play the part of a willing Asian ally to the US in its deepening involvement in Vietnam. President Johnson wanted the involvement of partner nations in his growing military engagement with communist forces. The initial ROK contribution was a mobile army surgical hospital and 130 personnel. In 1965, Park provided a two thousand personnel engineering unit to the American forces. As President Johnson continued to escalate a war effort in Vietnam, the Park administration added forces so that by the end of 1966, the top American commander had forty-five thousand ROK soldiers in Vietnam, more than from any other American ally (Jager, p. 345-346).

In 1965, Park took steps to open economic relations with Japan. Despite this being an unpopular move among the Korean constituency that remembered an oppressive Japanese occupation, Park wanted future benefits from grants, loans, technology, and trade with his more economically-developed neighbor. The US, heavily engaged with both the ROK and Japan, favored such a treaty. The two governments established normal diplomatic relations. The ROK, no longer a subject nation to Japan, would receive $800 million in grants and credits over ten years, settle some issues about fishing rights, and half a million Koreans living in Japan would receive legal status (Chapin, *New York Times*, October 5, 1965).

In 1966, the US signed a status of forces agreement with the Park administration that set a clear legal agreement between the ROK and the American military establishment.

Park and his government had achieved the kind of legal status with the United States that was in force with European NATO countries and Japan. This was a notable boost to national pride in Korea. In May 1967, Park Chung Hee won reelection by more than a million votes, defeating the same opponent as in 1963 but by a larger majority. The fairness of the election process was affirmed by the United Nations Commission for the Unification and Rehabilitation of Korea (Trumbull, *New York Times*, May 5, 1967). An Asian policy expert judged the American relationship with Park this way:

> The United States helped to pave the way by patient investment which kept this war-shattered nation supplied with food and other necessities, laid an infrastructure in a land almost devoid of natural resources, created educational opportunities, built several layers of experienced administrative personnel and ended Korea's international isolation. Political stability, painfully attained under the Park Chung Hee government after a period of crisis and strife, established a climate in which businessmen and others could look to the future, inflation could be checked and coordinated planning begun. Once the watershed was passed, momentum built up rapidly. Austerity and hard work paid off. Three years ago, the United States aid mission was expanding; now it is being rapidly reduced (Chapin, 1969).

Perhaps it was the Park administration's clear success in producing a rising economy in South Korea that provoked Kim Il Sung to strike a blow at Park. In January 1968, Kim dispatched a commando team into South Korea with the mission to assassinate Park.

> The thirty-one commandos were nearly on the doorsteps of the Blue House [the ROK presidential mansion] when they were found. In the ensuing firefight and pursuit, all the commandos were killed except one, who was later captured. Sixty-eight

ROK soldiers, policemen, and civilians and three American soldiers were killed in the hunt for the would-be assassins. Kim's gamble had backfired, as huge anti-North Korean demonstrations were mounted in Seoul and a wave of anti-communist hysteria swept through the country (Jager, pp. 372-373).

The North Koreans also provoked a conflict with the US when it captured an American intelligence ship in international waters in February 1968. The ship and its crew were held for nearly a year.

The North's refusal to release the *Pueblo* crew even led the Soviets, in bilateral discussions with Kim Il Sung, to advise him to lower tensions by ending the ordeal, since he had made his point and milked all the propaganda value from it already. The ten-month crisis finally ended in December 1968 with a written apology from the Johnson administration, which was later disavowed once the crew was returned (Cha, pp. 54-55; for a detailed account, see Lerner, *The Pueblo Incident*, 2002).

Kim's terrorism failed to undermine public confidence in Park or to provoke the South Koreans from maintaining strong ties to the protection afforded by a significant American presence in their country.

Despite continuing good relations between the ROK and the US, in 1972, President Park suspended constitutional government and imposed martial law on his country. Although Park's move was not popular with his political rivals, "Park justified his actions on the grounds that South Korea must be united and strong to deter or survive another North Korean attack" (Jager, p. 396). Jager notes that ordinary Koreans accepted Park's actions as an apt response to the issues of the time. The expiring Johnson administration in the US engaged in closed door dialogue about the change but judged it to be impractical to intervene. The matter was ignored and regarded as an internal Korean matter. That facilitated Park's modernization plans for the country to have its own reliable and productive heavy industries. In 1974, Park chose to undertake the development of nuclear technology, but, with opposing pressure from the US, that effort was put aside in 1976.

A dark side of the Park regime was its Korean Central Intelligence Agency (KCIA). "Acting through the KCIA, the Army Security Command, and his increasingly powerful personal security guards, Park sought to silence all those who interfered or disagreed with his policies by temporary detention, arrest, or imprisonment" (Oberdorfer and Carlin, pp. 33-34). When Jimmy Carter gained the American presidency in 1977, one of his priorities was to reduce the US military commitment, then about forty thousand troops, to South Korea. Carter criticized human rights abuses in South Korea by the Park regime. In an anti-democratic effort by the Park administration to oppose Carter's desire to pull back American troops, the KCIA funneled illegal gifts and campaign funds to members of the US Congress. According to the *Washington Post*, a Korean agent distributed bribes to "as many as 90 members of Congress and other officials" (Oberdorfer and Carlin, p. 73). There was a substantial disagreement within the Carter administration about the wisdom of such troop reductions and active opposition in Congress. Not successful in persuading the American policy establishment, Carter met with Park in the Blue House in 1979. There, Park argued to Carter that a troop withdrawal would be a tragic mistake, visibly angering Carter and providing him no Korean support for his withdrawal wishes. The result was face-saving for Carter; tiny withdrawal of fewer than seven hundred troops and a promise to revisit the issue in 1981. However, Carter lost the election in 1980, thus was unable to press his case from the American presidential bully pulpit.

Ironically, despite the fact that the KCIA had been a powerful instrument for control by Park, its director turned against him in 1979. A problem arose within Park's inner circle. The apparent issue was a combination of rivalry between the KCIA director and Park's head of Blue House security, as well as a matter of repressing dissent and opposition to Park's heavy-handed rule. Park's death by assassination "came not from the hands of a North Korean assassin, but from Kim Jae Kyu [not to be confused with Kim Il Sung or any other of the many Koreans named Kim], an original member of the revolutionary group that took power in May 1961 and one of Park's closest colleagues and advisers ... Subsequent investigations supported the conclusion that Park's murder was a crime of passion and not the result of a conspiracy" (Jager, p. 416).

After a chaotic time of rule by generals using martial law, Chun Doo Hwan resigned from the army to accept the appointment to the ROK presidency from the National Conference for Unification. He promised a new constitution and a future indirect election process for the presidency while administering the government on the basis of martial law. At the time

> What the Korean people think about all this is a complicated matter. Polls show that many people want democracy ... But there are forces in Korean society that make president Chun's task easier. The 600,000 men under arms are a major force in Korea ... Business support is also assured for Mr. Chun or any other strong leader who will keep the nation's nonunionized labor forces under control. The conservatism of the peasantry is another factor in Mr. Chun's favor. Centuries of Confucian tradition have made the attitude of the rural population one of allegiance to the ruler, whoever he may be ... The long-term future of the Chun administration appears assured ... and authoritarian rule, tougher than that of Mr. Park (Stokes, *New York Times*, September 22, 1980).

In the United States, the Carter administration was facing an election. After Carter's defeat, the Reagan administration embraced Chun and South Korea as a valued ally and welcomed him to the White House in February 1981. "The two presidents announced they would immediately resume previously postponed military and economic consultations ... Reagan's warm White House reception was a major turning point for Chun, convincing most South Koreans that his takeover was a fait accompli. By his action, Reagan built a store of obligation and goodwill with Chun that he [Reagan] drew upon later in connection with other issues" (Oberdorfer and Carlin, p. 108).

In 1986, Alan Romberg offered something of a mid-decade assessment about American concerns in the Asian nations for the prominent journal, *Foreign Affairs*. Regarding South Korea, he noted the continuing economic success under Chun that generated per capita GNP "from under $100 in 1960 to over $2,000 in 1985." Still there was uncertainty about the result of elections "in which the fledgling New Korea Democratic Party scored a stunning upset victory in the cities and garnered a solid minority bloc of seats [in the National Assembly]." Chun had cracked down on student demonstrators and punishments were imposed according to "severe national security laws rather than under normal criminal statutes." There was concern about whether or not Chun would step down at the end of his term in 1988. Addressing other American observers, Romberg cautioned:

> Long-term U.S. interests call for continuing support for political and economic liberalization [in South Korea], but not at a destabilizing pace. The impulse may be to favor full democracy now. But the realities of Korea suggest that resumption of the pre-May 1985 course should be the immediate goal, not withdrawal of support for Chun Doo Hwan, as student activists demand, or immediate revision of the constitution, as the opposition wants. Chun should be held to his promise of a peaceful transfer of power in 1988; in the meantime he should be encouraged to meet his nation's security concerns without resorting to the repressive measures his hard-line advisers have

successfully urged on him since last spring. But it would be feckless and even irresponsible for the United States to press a course that will inevitably lead to political retrogression and a stifling of economic dynamism (Romberg, *Foreign Affairs,* 1986).

Leading up to 1988, President Reagan and others in the US foreign-policy establishment offered repeated encouragement to Chun to step aside and provide for a free presidential election. Although Chun had previously averred that he would do so, his hold on the military establishment stirred fears among students and urban middle class careerists that Chun might hang on to the presidency or arbitrarily choose and impose a successor upon the people. In June 1987, Chun did call together party leaders of the Democratic Justice Party and requested the nomination of his political favorite and a former general, Roh Tae Woo. A prompt political convention of the party did follow Chun's choice and nominated Roh as its candidate. Chun's opponents mobilized hostile disapproval, fearing that another appointed executive was what Chun was trying to accomplish. Quickly, riots broke out in major cities with thousands of protesters fearful of a strongman grab for the presidency.

The American establishment prevailed upon President Reagan to make a strong president-to-president plea for Chun to make a peaceful exit from power and allow the transfer of the presidency to an elected, not an appointed, successor. The American ambassador to South Korea, James Lilley, insisted on personally delivering the Reagan letter while Chun was contemplating military moves against the protesters. Lilley made a forceful presentation of the American argument. "About an hour after Lilley left the Blue House, aides to Chun were told that the mobilization order had been suspended. Chun had put his sword back into the scabbard and turned to a political solution" (Oberdorfer and Carlin, p. 133). The result was actually a calm and orderly process of election in December 1987. In a genuine democratic turn-around, South Korea would get a president with an electoral mandate from the people in a free election.

CHAPTER 4: FOCUS ON NORTH KOREA

Who today would think

North Korea was the most industrial and urbanized Asian country to emerge from World War II. This was because Japan's occupation of Korea from 1910 to 1945 left massive industries in northern Korea. Colonial authorities built mines and processing plants for deposits of coal, iron, magnesium, and zinc, which were more plentiful in the north than in the south ... By 1945, when Korea was liberated by Soviet and U.S. troops, the northern half possessed 76 percent of the peninsula's mining production, 80 percent of its heavy industrial capacity, and 92 percent of its electricity-generating capabilities ... By contrast, in South Korea, which the Japanese treated as the 'bread basket' of the Korean colony, there was no industry to nationalize and only scorched rice paddies (Cha, p. 22).

After the armistice between the North and South in 1953, North Korea made remarkable early economic strides.

During the two plan periods following the conclusion of the Korean War, North Korea made economic advancement unequalled anywhere in the world. During the Three Year (Reconstruction) Plan of 1954-56, it claimed a 220% increase in national income and a 280% increase in gross industrial output. During the ensuing Five Year Plan of 1956-60 the comparable increases were, respectively, 210% and 340%. By 1960 national income reached 680% of the 1946 level while gross industrial product was 2100%. Substantial discounting of growth rates due to statistical inflation still makes for impressive results (Chung, p.528).

Kim Il Sung succeeded exceedingly well in the postwar era at cultivating friendship and economic support from the Soviet Union and the People's Republic of China. Large investments were made during the two earlier plans that focused on heavy industry. The Seven Year Plan undertaken in 1961 was supposed to take a more people oriented direction toward consumer goods and services. However, with hardening relationships by the communist countries toward the US, Kim turned attention to enlarging and equipping the North's military forces. Kim made disproportionately large investments in iron and steel plants, oil refineries, mining, and heavy machinery. These priorities necessitated putting the labor force into heavy industries and away from agricultural production and light manufacturing of consumer goods. The early 1960s were Cold War years, so the products of Kim's investment increasingly favored his military defense. Kim took pride in developing a fortress with nationalistic public pleas that aroused its citizenry to a willingness to bear arms. "In December 1962 the DPRK announced a four-point modernization program to: (1) arm the people; (2) modernize weaponry; (3) fortify the country; and (4) train each soldier ... The entire society was militarized for men from the ages of fifteen to forty-five and for women from eighteen to thirty-five" (Cha, p. 115). This strongly militaristic turn in priorities necessarily took the attention of the leadership and productivity of the workforce away from the production of consumer goods and human services.

Another huge distraction from domestic productivity was

the large commitments of time and energy by people at all levels to ideological indoctrination. The leading cadres were responsible for inculcating the ordinary citizens into dogmatic faith in the belief system and directional choices of the leaders of their country. The indoctrination of ordinary people was centered upon the cult of Kim Il Sung. A Western visitor reported in 1972 about elaborate study halls in all the towns, factories, and villages. Ordinary North Koreans were expected to discuss and accept the guidance "offered by the beloved and respected leader," Kim himself. Such study would impose upon the people two hours each day, plus four hours on Saturday. In primary schools, children would learn by heart and chant together aloud the great revolutionary ideas of Kim Il Sung (Byung, p. 146).

Economic analysis confirms that authentic economic success was achieved by the DPRK during the 1950s, but not sustained in the 1960s. The earlier advances may have led to an overestimation of the prospects for economic growth in the 1960s. Supposedly, the earlier emphasis on heavy industry was to be revised and the 1961 Seven Year Plan would raise the standard of living for the people by providing housing and consumer goods from light industry along with agricultural productivity gains that would enable more food supply and better diets (Cha, p. 150). However, the Seven Year Plan brought cruel disappointment, so much so that the leadership extended the effort for an additional three-year period.

> Since entering the Seven Year Plan in 1961 the pace of economic progress began to register a sharp decline ... Average annual rate of growth of national income declined from 21.0% during the Five Year Plan [1956-60] to 8.9% during the Seven Year Plan. Relative slowdown (as indicated by the index of slowdown) was even worse for the industrial output whose annual rate declined from 36.6% to 12.8%. In 1966 industrial output actually declined 3% over the preceding year, for the first time in North Korea. Thus, it is not surprising that

by 1970, three years after the initial target year of the Seven Year Plan, industrial output barely fulfilled its goal. The fact that no mention was made of the status of national income and agricultural output in Kim Il Sung's report to the Fifth Congress leads one to suspect that they were not fulfilled, omission being a major Communist technique for concealing poor performance.

Available data on the production of major industrial and agricultural products for 1960-1970 ... reveal that the slowdown is more serious than the impression received from the overall indicators discussed above. Not only did the rate of production slow down, but there were many instances of production reverses (current output falling below that of the previous period) covering all segments of the economy (heavy and light industry and agriculture) over several years. They affected such strategic products as iron ore, pig iron, steel, metal cutting machines, tractors, chemical fertilizers, textiles and rice. Since North Korea has withdrawn hitherto published important economic data (coinciding with its slowdown) and what scanty data it publishes tend to reflect favorable developments, the actual magnitude of the economic failures must be far more extensive and serious than the lowest possible level of production setbacks delineated by available announced data (Chung, pp. 528-529).

Certainty of the unproductive or unsuccessful economic choices for investment made by the DPRK foundered on ideological rigidities. The *juche* emphasis upon self-reliance by and among the North Korean people had both positive and negative consequences. It functioned well for building national pride and support for the entire social system. But it did not always apply well to the reality and limitations of the country's natural endowments. An illustrative case is about producing electrical power derived from hydropower plants.

Despite making a heavy investment in construction for water power, the consequent productivity was disappointing. Scientific advice suggested that a more dependable means would be thermal energy from petroleum. Oil on the world market in the 1960s was relatively inexpensive and widely available, but that was not the true way according to a published judgment in 1974 from the Great leader, Kim Il Sung. Two quotes illustrate Kim's rigidity.

> Certain scientists in former days suggested that oil-burning stations should be built, saying that oil-power stations can be built in less time than hydroelectric plants. That is true. However, if we build oil-burning stations, we will have to import oil from other countries, for it is not available in our country. This is contrary to our party's policy of building an independent economy. Therefore, I did not accept the scientists' suggestion and decided to build power stations that rely on the resources of our own country (Kim Il Sung, quoted by Cha, p. 114).

> A revealing commentary on the status of chuch'e [alternate spelling for *juche*] in North Korea was offered by Kim Il Sung in January 1974. In a speech to a national agricultural conference, he scolded cadres for failing to indoctrinate scientists and technicians properly. Deploring the low level of the latter's commitment to work, Kim urged cadres to tell scientists and technicians exactly what to do. 'Unless [they] are told unequivocally what problems to do research on and what books to read,' he said, 'they will not study diligently ... Today a sizable number of them are idling away their time' (Koh, footnote 44).

In a breakthrough event for Americans and the Red Chinese during February 1972, President Nixon went to China to meet with its leader, Mao Zedong. Kim Il Sung, perhaps reading the end of the Vietnam War and the then-warming relations between the United States and China as a signal that the US might be reducing its ties to South Korea, let it be known that contact with the Park Chung Hee regime in the South would be welcome. The cover story for leader-to-leader contact was a conference of the Red Cross that included spokespersons for both North and South Korea. At about the same time, South Korea's President Park expressed his concerns about the future steadiness of American support for South Korea. In 1971, President Nixon had reduced American troops in South Korea by about twenty thousand soldiers. In March 1972, Kim Il Sung received Park's director of the KCIA for private talks. The negotiations were conducted in secrecy. Surprising the South Koreans, Kim apologized for the attempt on Park's life by the North Korean commandos in 1968, although Kim did not acknowledge personal responsibility for it. The negotiation resulted in a publicized agreement between the North and South Korean regimes upon three principles which were announced on July 4, 1972.

First, unification shall be achieved through independent efforts without being subject to external imposition or interference.

Second, unification shall be achieved through peaceful means, not through use of force against one another.

Third, a great national unity, as a homogeneous people, shall be sought first, transcending differences in ideas, ideologies, and systems (Oberdorfer and Carlin, pp. 19- 20).

A long series of bilateral contacts followed that extended into 1975. Apparently, both leaders reaped benefits from the negotiation. World leaders elsewhere were encouraged to know that there were diplomatic meetings going on between the North and South. Washington applauded the apparent easing of tensions between the DPRK and the ROK as a positive change, and looked forward to more reductions of American troops along the 38th parallel. In late 1972, Park achieved popular approval of a new constitution by a national referendum. It enlarged his executive powers and provided for a National Conference for Unification that renewed Park's presidency for an additional six-year term. His capacity to push for greater economic development and greater independence from the US was enhanced. However, he harbored no genuine intentions to work toward unification with the North.

Kim's intent was to foster American intentions to reduce its troop commitment in the South. While seeming to make nice with the South, Kim successfully negotiated for diplomatic recognition from other countries around the world. "Immediately following the start of North-South dialogue, Pyongyang gained recognition from five Western European nations and many more neutral countries. Within four years, North Korea was recognized by ninety-three countries, on a par with South Korea's relations with ninety-six" (Oberdorfer and Carlin, p. 36). Kim's optimism was that a diminished US role in the South would allow the North's subversion and propaganda to successfully displace the Park regime to the North's benefit.

In time, the fruitless negotiations between the North and the South dried up, with neither side being able to accept the interests of the other. "Although both Kim and Park were in favor of unification, each was fiercely opposed to a merger on the other leader's terms. Without a strong push from the outside powers, who had conflicting interests and were paying little attention to the Korean Peninsula, the two rival states were incapable of sustaining their dialogue" (Oberdorfer and Carlin, p. 37). The major powers — the Soviet Union, the People's Republic of China, and the United States — were focused upon larger controversies among themselves, thus too preoccupied to overcome the improbable and delicate intricacies of diplomacy regarding South and North Korean stubbornness about unification.

Having opened diplomatic ties with many nations and seeming to be in peace negotiations with the South, the DPRK sought economic wellbeing through borrowing. "In fact, between 1970 and 1975, the North borrowed approximately $1.2 billion before foreign governments realized that Pyongyang could not service the debt ... Trapped by its own self-reliance ideology, the North could not do things normal nations would, such as issue bonds to finance its debt. Today [2012], North Korea's external debt is estimated at $12.5 billion and no one expects them to pay it off" (Cha, p. 117). Not included in these debt figures are loans and grants from various communist countries, particularly the Soviet Union and China.

By 1974, Kim returned to hardline tactics to weaken or create chaos in the ROK. In 1974, another North Korean assassin attempted to kill Park as he gave a speech on Korean Independence Day. The unsuccessful assassin's shots missed Park but killed his wife. Three months later, a routine ROK Army patrol near the 38th parallel discovered a sophisticated underground tunnel system extending under the demilitarized zone [DMZ] into South Korea. "The US command calculated that about 2,000 troops could be squeezed into the tunnel from its source, about two miles away in North Korea, to its planned exit south of the DMZ, and that additional troops could be put through at a rate of five to seven hundred men per hour. Suddenly, American and South Korean forces faced a threat of surprise attack behind their forward defense lines" (Oberdorfer and Carlin, p. 45). The discovery led to more systematic searching for similar large tunnels resulting in major discoveries in 1975, 1978, and 1990. The costly and sophisticated tunnel system constituted clear evidence of continuing hostile intentions by the DPRK and Kim Il Sung. During the 1980s, assassinations were attempted on the life of Park's successor, Chun Doo Hwan. While Chun was visiting Africa in 1982, a detailed assassination plot "was called off at the last minute because it was decided that an assassination in an African country would have squandered the North's much-valued, much-needed African support in the U.N. General Assembly." After that, "Chun narrowly escaped death when a terrorist bomb was planted by the North ... in Rangoon." The North Korean agents blew up the wrong car of the motorcade, killing half of Chun's cabinet ministers, but missing Chun (Cha, p. 57).

Revealed as a secretively hostile opponent to the South and an unreliable debtor nation, North Korea was increasingly dependent upon the Soviet Union and the People's Republic of China for help and assistance. During the 1970s and well into the 1980s, it was the Soviet Union that mostly sustained North Korea. China was dealing with its own turmoil during and after the disastrous Cultural Revolution, which lasted a decade - until 1976. China's economy suffered productivity losses, so it limited its relationships with other nations, including the DPRK. At that time, there was particular hostility between China and the Soviet Union, even skirmishes along their borders. Thus

> North Korea depended almost exclusively on the largess of the Soviet Union, which until 1984 provided more than $1 billion in foreign aid and credits annually, mostly in soft loans that Pyongyang did not repay ... The DPRK had fallen into a classic poverty trap. Stagnant economic growth stifled investments to grow the economy. The North's economy was degraded by a lack of innovation and by a dependence on imported raw materials with no resources to pay for them (Jaeger, pp. 429-430).

In 1982, the DPRK celebrated the Great Leader's seventieth birthday by erecting an arch of triumph in Pyongyang. According to the "Explore North Korea" website:

> It was built in April Juche 71 (1982) at the foot of Moran Hill to memorialize the triumphal return of President Kim Il Sung. 10,500 blocks of granite were piled up. It is 60m in height and 52.5m in width. The four columns were decorated by embossed images. And the years '1925' and '1945' carved in relief symbolize the years when the President embarked on revolution and liberated Korea. Carved in relief are the words of 'Song

of General Kim Il Sung'. (http://www.explorenorth-korea.com/arch-of-triumph.html)

Commentary in Western sources about North Korea's arch ridiculed it as a vanity effort because it was intentionally made to be somewhat larger the Parisian *Arc de Triomphe* that it emulates. Europeans insist it is simply "uglier." The lower half of the North Korean arch is Greco-Roman, but the top, or roof, lends a much more Asian appearance. The monument was built at the direction of Kim Il Sung's son, Kim Jong Il, who headed an agency known as the 4-15 Creation Group that established over twelve thousand monuments to his father (Cha, p. 79). By the beginning of the 1980s, Kim Il Sung had engineered the succession of his son, Kim Jong Il, to become the next leader, to be known as the "Dear Leader." Curiously, such a succession was taboo in communist countries around the world and that included North Korea.

> The 1970 edition of the Dictionary of Political Terminologies, published by Pyongyang's official Academy of Social Science, under the heading of 'Hereditary Succession' had renounced succession by heredity of certain 'riches and positions' as a 'reactionary custom of exploitative systems of the old days ...still practiced in the capitalist societies as a means to dominate the working class.' The whole paragraph together with the heading, however, was deleted in the updated Political Dictionary, 1972 edition, published on 31 December 1973, by the same institution under the name of 'Social Science Publishing House.' This was obviously a clear indication of North Korea's change of mind on the succession issue (Kim and Lee, p. 259).

Kim Il Sung was able to change orthodox Marxism and the rhetoric of the Korean Workers' Party. On the occasion of the Party's thirtieth anniversary, its textbook for its cadre referred to Kim Jong Il as the "exclusive successor" to his father (Kim and Lee, p. 264). While Western observers have been scornful of North Korea and its deficiencies, Kim II Sung's political skills allowed him to exercise supreme power for more than forty years, until his death on July 8, 1994. No other communist leader had such longevity, nor could any command the authority to successfully replace himself with his son.

The evidence of economic decline became apparent in the late 1980s. Despite the ideology of *juche*, North Korea suffered for its dependence on the Soviet Union when the Soviet Union and the Warsaw Pact it sponsored went into decline. Eberstadt has described a disparate scenario when making the comparison between the two Koreas.

> Thereafter—with the revolutions of 1989 in eastern Europe and the crisis of the Soviet state—the North Korean economy was shaken by an unexpected dislocation. With the end of the Soviet bloc North Korea's trade with these former allies collapsed. Since the advent of hard currency terms of payment last year, for example, the former Soviet Union has all but ceased exporting to North Korea. Just before its dissolution the Warsaw Pact had accounted for well over half of North Korea's trade turnover. The sudden end to this commerce has been devastating. It has deprived North Korea of both its foreign markets for low quality machinery and consumer goods, and of the spare parts and equipment necessary to keep Soviet bloc facilities and infrastructure functioning.

> In theory Pyongyang could cope with this particular crisis by turning toward market-oriented economies. But North Korea has already poisoned its commercial relations with Western countries by its default on international loans in the 1970s and its intransigence with private creditors ever since. In effect North Korea is reduced to bartering for goods on the world market, and there is little scope for expanding such activities under current

circumstances (Eberstadt, *Foreign Affairs,* Winter 1992/93).

Coincident with North Korea's economic decline in the 1980s was a rise in Kim Il Sung's interest in nuclear energy development. According to Jaeger, Kim first lobbied the Soviet Union for development of a nuclear power plant during the 1960s and 1970s, but the Kremlin considered North Korea too unreliable an ally to receive such a costly and controversial type of foreign assistance. "The DPRK made another request in 1976, even as contentious negotiations over North Korea's debt were taking place in Moscow" (Jager, p. 434). However, the international setting changed in the 1980s as the Sino-American relationship warmed and the relationships of the Soviet Union with both the United States and China cooled. "North Korea's strategic importance to the Soviet Union increased ... The Soviet Union thus agreed to supply for LWRs [light water reactors] in 1985, but only if North Korea had joined the NPT [Non-Proliferation Treaty], which it did in December of that year. The NPT required signatories to sign a safeguard inspection agreement within eighteen months that permitted inspections to identify violations" (Jager, p. 435).

After the Soviet Union welched on its promised reactors, North Korea went ahead on its own. Photos from American surveillance satellites detected the construction of a nuclear plant in Yongbyon.

> In March 1984, as construction proceeded, a satellite pass showed the outline of a cylindrical nuclear smokestack rising from the site ... But in June 1988, construction for a much larger reactor, eventually described by the North Koreans as intended to produce 50 megawatts of power, was photographed at Yongbyon. Such a plant, in combination with the huge reprocessing facility under construction, convinced most Washington officials ... that North Korea was launched headlong on a drive to create its own nuclear weapons (Oberdorfer and Carlin, p. 194-195).

Initially, US intelligence about the DPRK's nuclear developments was a narrowly held secret. However, for international purposes, the newly-elected president, George H. W. Bush, chose to notify Soviet and Chinese officials in order to gain backing for multinational pressure to bring about inspections and to limit North Korea's nuclear capability to peaceful purposes only. The United States likewise warned South Korea and Japan about American concerns regarding a nuclear program in North Korea. The resulting publicity prompted the DPRK mission at the United Nations to put out a denial, "an utterly groundless lie," about any nuclear weapons activity.

The United States' desire to prevent the DPRK from developing nuclear weapons eventually generated wide consequences. The US wanted the International Atomic Energy Agency (IAEA) to conduct inspections in North Korea to prevent any weaponization of nuclear materials in North Korea. The IAEA, organized in 1957, was created with the objective of guiding "atoms for peace" in nations around the world. It would do so by promoting safe, secure, and peaceful use of nuclear technologies. However, to prove its peaceful purposes on the Korean Peninsula, the Bush administration took steps to eliminate the American nuclear weapon footprint in South Korea. By December 1991, American nuclear weapons – artillery and bombs – were removed from South Korea. Bush assured the then South Korean president, Roh Tae Woo, that the US would provide the ROK with nuclear protection but the weapons would not be located in the country. Moreover, Bush would permit North Korean inspectors to scrutinize a US base in Kunsan where such weapons had previously been stored. President Roh publicly announced the weapons removal in an official communiqué to his people and the rest of the world (Oberdorfer and Carlin, p. 202).

The point of the Bush withdrawal of nuclear weapons and the offer of inspections was to achieve agreement with the DPRK to submit to inspections in the North. Helpful pressure on the DPRK came from China. By 1991, China was increasingly open to trade around the world and the US had quickly become a major trade partner. China was supportive of the entry by both North Korea and South Korea into the United Nations. Meanwhile, China was in enlarging its trade relations with the ROK, and it encouraged the DPRK toward reconciliation with South Korea. Kim Il Sung responded to the pressure and the ROK's initiative from President Roh. In 1991, the two Koreas hammered out guidelines for an interim relationship headed toward an authentic peace agreement. "On December 24, at a North Korean Workers' Party Central Committee plenum, Kim Il Sung praised the recent North-South nonaggression pact ... [and] ended with a public report that contained no criticism of South Korea or the United States" (Oberdorfer and Carlin, p. 205). At that time, the Party named Kim's son, Kim Jong Il, as his designated successor and the supreme commander of the DPRK's military. The Party also approved, in principle, that the DPRK's nuclear facilities would become subject to international inspection.

There was no American or ROK objection to the peaceful use of nuclear power in North Korea. But there was concern about the possibility of reprocessing waste from spent reactor fuel into plutonium, a basic material for nuclear weapons. Based upon satellite surveillance, US military intelligence was highly suspicious that North Korea had reprocessing capability. Kim Il Sung insisted to a visiting American congressman, "We have no nuclear reprocessing facilities" (Oberdorfer and Carlin, p. 206). Desiring inspections, the US and ROK canceled routine military exercises, known as Team Spirit, in order to please the DPRK. In return, the US called for North Korea's agreement regarding reciprocal inspections of facilities in both the North and South. There was a celebration after both sides signed an agreement on December 31, 1991, not to test, produce, or use nuclear weapons and not to reprocess nuclear material for possible weapons. Both sides agreed to allow inspections of nuclear facilities. The follow-up to that agreement in January 1992 was North Korea's acceptance of membership in the International Atomic Energy Agency (IAEA), which was ratified in North Korea the following April. This was the high point in the prospect that North Korea would not threaten international peace by means of nuclear weapons.

In 1992, North Korea admitted IAEA inspectors in May and July. Sophisticated testing of radioactive waste revealed evidence that North Korea was capable of reprocessing the waste, fueling fears both in South Korea and the US that North Korea could and would weaponize the reprocessed waste. The hoped-for normalization of relationships with the DPRK slowed down. The ROK wanted the US to restart their joint Team Spirit military exercises that had been canceled in order to please the DPRK previously. The budding relationships of North Korea with the South and the US turned into feelings of distrust. As the IAEA inspectors continued to monitor, gather evidence, and interpret their findings, they concluded that North Korea had undeclared nuclear waste sites. When the IAEA demanded visits to the sites, North Korea stalled. When Hans Blix, the IAEA director, presented data to member representatives confirming the likelihood of North Korea cheating on the agreement, there was international support for Blix's demands to conduct inspections of the two sites that had been kept from scrutiny. Blix notified the DPRK of the IAEA's request to examine the two sites in March 1993.

Instead of complying, Kim Jong II, North Korea's military leader, declared a state of readiness for war and unilaterally announced the DPRK's intent to withdraw from the Non-Proliferation Treaty. "As cover for its NPT withdrawal, Pyongyang gave two reasons: Team Spirit, which it charged had violated the spirit of the NPT and of the North-South denuclearization accord, and the IAEA demand for special inspection of two suspects sites, which it described as 'an undisguised strong-arm act designed to disarm the DPRK and strangle our socialist system' " (Oberdorfer and Carlin, p. 218).

This provoked a war of words involving China, the United States, the ROK, and the DPRK. Continuing negotiations were complicated by the fact that there were presidential administration turnovers in both South Korea and the United States, with Kim Young Sam succeeding Roh, and Bill Clinton succeeding George H. W. Bush. By June 1993, North Korea suspended its intention to withdraw from the Non-Proliferation Treaty in return for being allowed direct negotiations with the US. That stirred concern in the ROK and its new president, Kim Young Sam. The South Koreans were suspicious of possible bilateral agreements between the North and the United States that might conflict with South Korean interests. In the meantime, the IAEA insisted that North Korea still had not opened itself to inspection of its existing facilities. The new Clinton administration set forth its own proposed set of agreements.

> The essence of the immediate bargain was North Korean resumption of regular IAEA inspections and a renewal of dialogue with the South, in return for cancellation of the 1994 Team Spirit military exercise and the convening of a long-delayed third round of US-DPRK negotiations. [Later consultation] would deal with IAEA inspections of two disputed Yongbyon waste sites, diplomatic recognition North Korea, and trade and investment concessions from the United States, South Korea, and Japan (Oberdorfer and Carlin, p. 231).

The Clinton administration was surprised to learn that its offer to North Korea stirred opposition from Kim Young Sam's South Korean administration.

The next effort from the US was American pressure in the United Nations for Security Council-imposed sanctions on the North, but China would not agree to any sanctions. China feared that any destabilization of the DPRK would result in refugees flooding over the borders into China and Russia. "No one in the region wanted to upset the fragile balance of power on the Korean Peninsula and risk another conflict. This was the dilemma that the Clinton administration faced when Kim Il Sung raised the ante and precipitated a showdown that would lead the United States and North Korea to the brink of war" (Jager, p. 438).

After a DPRK announcement that it would change fuel rods in its nuclear reactor contrary to IAEA requirements, a frustrated Clinton administration contemplated the prospect that North Korea soon could turn its spent fuel into actual nuclear weapons. In June 1994, American planners provided Clinton with military options for bombing the North Korean facilities. In a dramatic moment in the defense advisers meeting with Clinton, a call was received at the White House from former United States President Jimmy Carter, who, speaking as a private citizen, had directly discussed issues with Kim Il Sung, who promised Carter he would freeze the North's nuclear program. Kim agreed not to change the fuel rods and weaponize the spent fuel rods. On that basis, Carter announced this news publicly and expressed opposition to sanctions against Pyongyang. Moreover, Carter suggested the prospect of his bringing about one-on-one negotiations between the presidents of North and South Korea. In the context of the favorable publicity received by former President Carter, "the sanctions activity and plans for extensive reinforcement of US troops were dropped. After obtaining written confirmation from Pyongyang of its acceptance of the US-devised freeze on its nuclear program, Washington announced readiness to proceed to the third round of US-DPRK negotiations, which were scheduled to begin on July 8 in Geneva" (Oberdorfer and Carlin, p. 263).

The sudden death of Kim Il Sung on July 8, 1994, brought a pause in negotiations but the talks did resume in August. The North Korean negotiators had a nuclear program in place that obviously worried the Asian neighbors and the US enough to drive a hard bargain for benefits. The "Agreed Framework," as the Clinton administration called it, promised North Korea a great deal.

- The DPRK would get two light water reactors for its future energy needs, along with a supply of heavy fuel oil to meet current energy needs.

- The DPRK would freeze nuclear development, submit to IAEA inspections and give up its spent fuel rods. Existing nuclear facilities would be eliminated when replaced by the LWRs.

- Trade barriers would be reduced in diplomatic relations normalized and the US would assure DPRK protection against nuclear weapons (Oberdorfer and Carlin, pp. 279-280).

The North Koreans took the agreement as a victory. It was a positive accomplishment for Kim Jong Il and it was received as a negotiated victory of the North over the South because it was a bilateral agreement between the DPRK and the US. Moreover, the DPRK had given up little to receive substantial and generous promises of aid and trade.

The Clinton administration had bought a relaxation of tensions with the North, but at the cost of offending the ROK because it was affected by, but not a participant, in the agreement. The agreement was a political liability for the Clinton administration, pushed as it was by former President Carter. Opinions in the American press viewed the Agreed Framework a giveaway of dubious value to the US. The agreement was only an executive agreement, not a treaty, because of its questionable approvability by Congress. That approvability declined even further when the 1994 election put the Republicans into a majority in both the House and the Senate.

Despite criticisms of the Agreed Framework, the US initiated shipments of heavy oil to North Korea and made slow progress creating the Korean Peninsula Energy Development Organization (KEDO), which was tasked particularly to provide the light water reactors for North Korea's nuclear powered electricity generation. Because the reactors would be provided by the ROK, there were issues of national pride – saving face – between the two Koreas, but the US managed to smooth ruffled feathers on each side of the 38th parallel.

During the 1990s, North Korea had extreme domestic problems but its leaders successfully initiated a missile program, and constituted another threat to its neighbors and the US. The US initiated a three-way alliance with the ROK and Japan to neutralize the DPRK's missile development. In 1999, the US offered North Korea a positive track, "leading step-by-step to full diplomatic, political, and economic relations with the United States. To obtain these benefits, North Korea must completely halt all missile exports, including related technology and equipment [and] North Korea must cease development, production, testing, and deployment of all missiles above the limit of the international [community]" (Oberdorfer and Carlin, p. 329).

Within months, the DPRK agreed to temporarily stop missile tests but the relationship did not develop further until 2000. The then South Korean president, Kim Dae Jong, initiated an effort to meet with Kim Jong II that resulted in a summit meeting in June. That meeting produced an agreement to move toward a reunified Korea through careful dialogue. After that, there were trade mission meetings, exchanges between hundreds of separated families, and even a joint march of ROK and DPRK athletes at the 2000 Olympics in Australia. In October, the North Korean negotiator to the US asked that President Clinton visit Pyongyang for direct talks. American Secretary of State Madeleine Albright promptly made the trip to find a very agreeable Kim Jong II. "Suddenly, the prospect of nearly limitless agreement had opened up at the eleventh hour of the Clinton administration, with only two weeks to go before the election of a new president and less than three months before Clinton would leave office. Although many concessions and promises had been outlined by Kim Jong II, most details remained to be worked out" (Oberdorfer and Carlin, p. 345).

The window for agreement was open too briefly to produce an enduring agreement. Neither side could hammer out the details before the end of the Clinton presidency. Moreover,

the outcome of the American presidential contest pro-
duced a partisan turnover from the Democrats to the
Republicans. The election outcome was in doubt until a
Supreme Court decision on December 12, 2000. After
that, the president-elect, George W. Bush, was skeptical
about making concessions to North Korea. Issues on the
Korean Peninsula were not high on the agenda of the new
Republican administration and there was little trust in the
worthiness of pursuing the Clinton administration's Agreed
Framework. For the time being, the matter of getting along
with the DPRK was left to the leaders of the ROK and
Japan.

CHAPTER 5: CHANGE THROUGH DEMOCRATIZATION IN SOUTH KOREA

It is beyond question that the Park and Chun administrations brought remarkable productivity to South Korea, along with economic and social benefits to its people. But democracy? That was another matter entirely. The immediate issue as Chun's presidency was coming to a close in 1987 was how would a successor be chosen and who would it be?

The democratization question was not at issue only in South Korea. Beginning in the 1970s, the world was caught up in what is widely acknowledged as the "third wave" of democratization (Huntington, 1991). It reached a high point in the late 1980s, as the communist dictatorships of Eastern Europe disintegrated and democracies began to emerge. An Asian awakening occurred in the Philippines when its people ousted Ferdinand Marcos in 1986, a "people power" revolution pursued with American encouragement. It was an apt time for popular change to break out in South Korea.

Democratic ideas and ideals were widely ascendant. With them came liberalization of civic life – expanding freedoms for people and groups. That included freedom for political dissent, a free press, and freedom of assembly. Democratization would go further, necessitating that governments be subject to the will of the people, all the people, by means of free and regular elections that offered competing candidates.

A unique accomplishment of the Chun administration played into the political context as the matter of democratization edged forward. One of Chun's closest supporters, Roh Tae Woo, who assisted Chun when he came to power after the Park assassination, was a prominent player in the accomplishment. After serving Chun as minister of home affairs, Chun appointed Roh to the chairmanship of South Korea's Olympic Committee. The Olympic Games, if brought to South Korea, would advance the nation's standing on the world stage. Roh was a key person in successfully convincing the International Olympic Committee to bring the Olympic Games to Seoul in 1988. As the Chun government prepared for the Games' worldwide press and television coverage, it needed civic peace. That required relative harmony among the citizenry, especially the volatile student demonstrators who were always alert for any backtracking by the Chun administration about future elections for a successor.

In June 1987, Chun announced that Roh Tae Woo should be the presidential nominee of the then ruling Democratic Justice Party. The party promptly complied with Chun's choice. But that move was widely perceived by dissidents around the country as an illegitimate effort to preempt the democratic process of choice by the people. "[M]assive, violent protests erupted across the country, spreading to more than 30 cities ... Tens of thousands of protesters were arrested" (Oberdorfer and Carlin, p. 130). After a chaotic couple of weeks and some indecision by President Chun, President Ronald Reagan counseled Chun against any violent crackdown against the demonstrators. "On June 29, Roh stunned Koreans by accepting the central demand for direct election of the next president – a daring move in view of the unpopularity of the ruling party" (Oberdorfer and Carlin, p. 134). Peace was restored and progress toward democratic change moved forward.

The period from late June through December 1987

saw the rapid implementation of political reforms in an unusual move of compromise between the ruling and opposition parties. In July the government paroled 357 political offenders, amnestied more than 2000 other prisoners, and restored full political rights to prominent opposition figure Kim Dae Jung. In August the National Assembly established a committee to study constitutional revision. Representatives of four parties took one month to negotiate and propose a draft constitution that incorporated most of the provisions long sought by the opposition: greater press freedom and protection for civil rights, a stronger National Assembly, and direct presidential elections. After the bill passed the National Assembly, more than 93 percent of the voters approved the new draft on October 28, 1987 (Savada and Shaw, pp. 215-216).

On December 16, 1987, the ROK conducted the first direct presidential election in sixteen years. In addition to Roh, the two main opposition candidates were Kim Dae Jung and Kim Young Sam. Although similar in their opposition to Roh, neither would step aside for the other. Roh became the beneficiary of the campaign resources of the incumbent president and the Democratic Justice Party. In the multi-candidate race, Roh received 36.9 percent of the vote: Kim Young Sam received 28 percent and Kim Dae Jung got 26.9 percent. The remaining eight percent went to two minor candidates (Savada and Shaw, p. 218). Although Roh won only a plurality, the political arena had provided an open contest between Roh and serious rivals. Given freedom of choice at the polls, the Korean people made their electoral preferences clear. The total turnout exceeded twenty-three million voters. Roh's selection came by means of a direct election process. Suffrage was universal, votes were of equal weight, and votes were cast as secret ballots. Voting turnout was 89.2 percent of the nearly twenty-six million registered voters (Croissant, p. 266). The evident propriety of the electoral process provided Roh substantial political legitimacy. Roh's election entitled him to one term (five years) in South Korea's presidential office. The one-term limit remains to this day as a significant constitutional check on ROK presidents.

Croissant has summarized the specifics of how the presidential electoral process firmed up in the succeeding elections of 1992 and 1997.

> Under the so called 'grand compromise' in 1990, the DJP (led by Roh Tae-woo), the Reunification Democratic Party (RDP - led by Kim Young-sam) and the New Democratic Republican Party (NDRP - led by Kim Jong-pil) merged to create the Democratic Liberal Party (DLP). The specific path taken by the transformation process and transformation strategies of the relevant decision makers thus had a stabilizing effect on the basic democratic institutions and procedures in the country. This was seen clearly when Kim Young-sam, then the candidate of the governing party, became the first civilian to assume the country's highest national and governmental office in 1992/93 after more than 30 years of military domination of national politics (Croissant, p. 243).

Despite the institutional instability of the political party organizations, they fluidly moved with their leading candidates, and the principles of free and open elections decided by the people became firmly established.

Another way of looking at South Korean democratization is revealed by survey research that examined what the authors called "two domains of support for democratization." They found that support for both increased over time, but noted that "Koreans' avowed *desire* for democracy is consistently higher than their assessment of democracy's *suitability* for the country." Identically-sized surveys were taken for each leadership regime, from Chun's pre-democratic selection to the elected government of Kim Young

Sam, and the data is summarized here:

Variations in Types of Support for Democratization across Three Governments

Types		Governments		
Desirability	Suitability	Chung 1980-1988	Roh 1988-93	Kim 1993-98
No	No	20.0	12.0	5.1
No	Yes	5.9	4.7	2.8
Yes	No	45.9	41.3	21.0
Yes	Yes	28.2	42.0	71.1
		100.0	100.0	100.0

Take note of the authors' interpretation of the data:

> [C]hanges in democratic support by tracking the combinations of personal preference and judgments of suitability across three government periods. A plurality (46 percent) assert that while they personally favored democratization in the authoritarian period [under Chun], they declined to endorse it then for the nation. By the time of the first democratic government [under Roh], a plurality (42 percent) favored democracy as a personal preference and viewed it as suitable for the nation. During the second democratic government [under Kim Young-sam], a large majority (71 percent) had become both personally and 'collectively' supportive of democracy. Thus, over the seven years of democratization in Korea, the number of those who saw democracy is both desirable and feasible increased by two and a half times, from 28 to 71 percent. Conversely, the fraction of those neither personally nor nationally supportive of change fell sharply, from twenty to five percent. As democracy took hold, negative dispositions toward democratization turned positive more readily than positive attitudes turned negative (Shin and McDonnell, pp. 13 – 14).

Unfortunately for South Korea, having progressed greatly in economic terms, first under authoritarian leaders and then under elected presidents, the country ran into an economic crisis in 1997-98. Despite national economic growth at a rate of seven percent or more a year, South Korea's large corporate conglomerates (referred to as chaebols) engaged in reckless borrowing to fund corporate expansion. When repayments on loans slowed, international investors in the Korean economy began to lose confidence and withdraw their capital investments. In short order, panic ensued in the world's financial markets. Although the panic broadly affected economies in South Asia, the Korean circumstance – with its hostile boundary at the 38th parallel, where there were some forty thousand American soldiers – received great notice in the United States. The panic, of course, had multiple causes. A careful analysis suggested three major developments that triggered the crisis. The first was the currency exchange rate. During the 1990s, the value of the US dollar rose and, in fact, altered values in the Korean economy.

> Consequently, as the dollar became stronger against the Japanese yen, Korea not only experienced an accelerated increase in its trade deficit, but also a severe drop in the profitability of investments undertaken for exports in particular. Some large business conglomerates ran into financial difficulties around this time and non-performing loans (NPLs) at Korean banks sharply increased, thus undermining the financial soundness of domestic banking institutions (Kim Kihwan, p. 7).

A specific issue was the debt problems at several of the great chaebols of South Korean industry, particularly the Hanbo group and Kia. Both were counting on the Korean government for bail outs. But the government refused, accentuating fears among foreign investors. Thirdly, as the financial contagion spread to Hong Kong and elsewhere, the Korean government used up its limited foreign-currency reserves to shore up Korean banks. But just as the economic peril increased, the national elections were at hand.

Afraid of possible adverse effects of passing such

a reform package on the forthcoming presidential election, however, all the political parties, including the Democratic Liberals, the party then in power, refused to act on the reform package. This was literally the proverbial last straw that broke the camel's back. The withdrawal of foreign funds accelerated even more, forcing the government to officially request help from the IMF [International Monetary Fund] on November 21 [1997] (Kim Kihwan, p. 10).

What was the effect of the economic crisis upon the democratization of the ROK? There was a negative consequence in the short term. Opinion surveys detected change: "As compared to the pre-crisis period, Koreans are now significantly less supportive of democracy as a normative as well as empirical phenomenon than for the crisis ... However, most people do not want to restore the old regime of military or civilian dictatorship" (Kim and Shin, p. 181). What the crisis did do, coming right before the December 1997 presidential election, was produce a significant electoral turn. "As a result, the Kim Young Sam government, not the democratic political system, became rapidly unpopular and delegitimized during the crisis period. Because the ruling party's legitimacy and popularity were also seriously undermined, the opposition candidate, Kim Dae Jung, won the Korean presidency in the 1997 elections" (Kim and Shin, pp. 246-247).

Kim Dae Jung's election brought about a successful and peaceful partisan turnover, although his political party, the National Congress for New Politics, had only a minority in the National Assembly. The ROK did make a swift economic recovery, not only reestablishing prosperity but extinguishing nostalgia for the kind of authoritarianism through which the Park regime had gotten the economy going a generation earlier. Kim brought to his presidency the conviction that South Korea needed parallel development of both its democratic processes, as well as in its market economy. His administration made corporate enterprises, the chaebols, more transparent. The reforms imposed on the corporate groups called for better reported corporate accounting and controls over non-bank financial institutions. The prompt financial recovery in the country confirmed that economic progress and democratic political processes could go forward in South Korea at the same time.

> Since the crisis, the success of the reforms – and the state's bid to regain legitimacy in the political economy – also benefited from the Kim government's ability to capitalise on the public's sense of outrage at the excesses of the chaebols and their culpability in the outbreak of the crisis. That is, the legitimacy that was restored to the state stemmed from two sources: the external support of the US and the IFIs [international financial institutions: for example. The International Monetary Fund] for implementing the neo-liberal agenda, and also domestic groups other than the chaebols. The government was more than willing to capitalise on the perception that the chaebols were responsible for bringing the economic crisis to the country due to their reckless lending and expansion. Thus the state gained public support for reining in, rather than nurturing, the chaebols – in contrast to the initial stages of economic development (Hundt, p.257).

Another noteworthy effort by Kim Dae Jung was referred to as his Sunshine Policy. Despite previous hostility from the DPRK, Kim's Sunshine Policy was an effort to engage in direct talks between the two Koreas. Despite the DPRK's initiatives regarding offensive nuclear weapons and missiles to deliver them, it was well known in the South that famine in the DPRK was causing widespread starvation there. The ROK's Kim took the initiative in January 2000 by proposing a summit meeting "to discuss issues of mutual cooperation, peaceful coexistence and coprosperity" (Oberdorfer and Carlin, p. 333). Efforts were set in motion to bring about top level meetings. The ROK's Kim even responded to press interviewers with compliments about Kim Jong Il's knowledge and good judgment. After a variety of contacts and discussions between lower-level leaders on both sides, the two Kims met in Pyongyang in June for three days of talks. They agreed that the South and North would work together to promote "reunification," allow exchange visits for separated family members, start economic and cultural exchanges, and to continue future meetings and dialogue between the leaders on both sides. When the ROK's Kim returned home, he credited the DPRK's Kim for a productive meeting. Success "was due in large measure to [Kim Jong Il's] ability to be receptive to new ideas and a willingness to change his views" (Oberdorfer and Carlin, p. 338).

In a gradual way, negotiations between the two Koreas picked up. There were a limited number (a hundred families on each side) of family reunions, commercial exchanges, and even the joint march of North and South Korean athletes at the 2000 Sydney Olympics. But the 2000 election in the United States brought George W. Bush and a new American administration into office. Bush and his team were highly skeptical about peaceful progress with North Korea. There was diplomatic engagement between the US and the DPRK, but in 2002, the American negotiators came to a high level discussion believing the DPRK was engaged in a uranium enrichment program that violated the Agreed Framework put in place with the Clinton administration. Not receiving a convincing denial from the DPRK negotiators, the Americans went away, confirmed in the view that North Korea cheated on its agreement with the US with a uranium enrichment program that could sustain weaponization. With that rationale, the US stopped the shipment of heavy fuel oil to North Korea for power generation. The DPRK responded by ceremoniously, publicly, and provocatively restarting its nuclear reactor in Yongbyon, which had been idle since 1994, a move regarded in the US and South Korea as a hostile North Korean response. Thus the Agreed Framework was dead, and the foundation for Kim Dae Jung's Sunshine Policy was undermined, never again to be reestablished.

Given the turbulence in South Korea (the ups and downs in the economy, the reforms imposed upon the chaebols, peaceful initiatives made to the North that were met with mixed responses in return), what was happening in regard to the democratization of the South Korean people? Survey data gathered during Kim Dae Jung's presidency is quite revealing. By this time, the nation had experienced three democratically-elected presidential administrations, including a peacefully accomplished partisan turnover with the election of Kim Dae Jung. This aroused scholarly interest in the depth of attachment to democratic beliefs and practices among the South Korean people. The major concern was whether South Korea could be judged a "consolidated" democracy. Would the people give evidence of "broad, deep, unconditional mass support for democratic institutions, processes and values ...? [Would they support a] culture of democracy ... not only accepting democracy, but rejecting its alternatives" (Shin and Wells, p. 89)?

The inquiry began by investigating the desirability of democracy, its suitability for the country, and the extent to which it was preferred over the authoritarian governments the South Korean people had previously experienced. The survey data revealed that nearly nine in ten respondents thought democracy to be "desirable" and "suitable," but just half considered it "preferable." There remained a measure of vulnerability in the affections of the people for authoritarian rule. However, when pressed about approval for the various forms of authoritarian governments (military, one party, or civilian), levels of approval varied from only ten to fifteen percent of the people. In contrast, about three-fourths rejected any of the kinds of nondemocratic regimes. When asked to evaluate the democratic processes of government, support for being governed in a democratic fashion was generally expressed by about two-thirds of the respondents: a political leader should follow established rules, compromise is appropriate, and respect for minority rights is necessary.

Negative views were expressed on related matters: even in a difficult situation, the government should not disregard the law; in judicial cases, judges should not feel bound by the chief executive's point of view; and censorship of ideas and speech should not be accepted. Across the range of governing practices, the democratic approach had wide approval from the South Korean people by a margin of two-to-one. When asked about approval for democracy in the abstract, the response was favorable at a nine-to-one ratio. The authors underscored their findings as follows: "We conclude that [in South Korea] democracy is indeed the only game in town, and that the political culture has completed its transformation from authoritarian to democratic ... [South Korea is] well on the way to [democratic] consolidation" (Shin and Wells, p. 99).

A particular concern related to democratization in South Korea was with regard to the matter of attachment to political parties. In democracies around the world, partisan attachments shape the attitudes, beliefs, and political behavior not only of the politicians contesting for office but also ordinary citizens as they engage in elections and pursue group interests. Partisanship expected to help engender citizen confidence in democratic governments. If this is true, partisan engagement will continue to sustain favorable attitudes toward democratic attachment – both in its ideals and practices.

In South Korea, as elsewhere, partisan attachment is variable among citizenry. In a Korean survey (Shin and Tusalem, 2007) conducted during the Kim Dae Jung presidency, only about a quarter of the respondents did not identify with a party (nonpartisan), while 38 percent were on the winning party side, and 35 percent on the losing party side. When distinguished this way, nearly half the nonpartisans (44 percent) and the losing partisans (49 percent) perceived their democracy as functioning well. Nearly two-thirds (65 percent) of the winning partisans viewed their democracy as well functioning. When asked about opposition to authoritarian rule, large majorities in each category (winning partisans, 68 percent; losing partisans, 71 percent; nonpartisans, 77 percent) expressed such a position. The authors concluded that mass partisanship had contributed to democratization in the ROK and had enhanced the rejection of authoritarian appeals. The consolidation of democracy, never utterly complete and total, was moving definitely and positively in an affirmative direction in the ROK as the twenty-first century was getting underway.

The ROK's next presidential election took place in December 2002, ending the Kim Dae Jung administration. The race for the ROK presidency was a close one. The polling favorite in the contest, a patrician conservative who lost to Kim Dae Jung five years earlier, was Lee Hoi-chang, who garnered 47 percent of the vote. The winner, however, was Roh Moo Hyun, Kim Dae Jung's faithful supporter. An underdog, he surged at the end of the campaign to a narrow victory with 49 percent of the electorate's support. His party, the Millennium Democratic Party, was Kim's party as well.

Roh, born to a humble farming family, did not attend college but through self-education, he achieved admission to the bar as a lawyer. He was a human rights advocate, first losing, then winning, a seat in the National Assembly. He was popular among young, college-educated voters, supported by the so-called "386 Generation," people mostly in their forties or younger. In contrast with Lee, who was generally closely aligned with the Americans in military issues and relationships with the DPRK, Roh took a more independent stance. "Roh's commitment to engagement with North Korea, the most important legacy of his political mentor, President Kim, has been so pronounced at times that it produced a stunning last-minute turn of events that many here thought could have cost him the election" (French, *New York Times*, December 20, 2002). That stance was clear when he suggested that his administration might be neutral in a possible confrontation between the US and the DPRK. Roh opposed the traditional authoritarianism of Korea's earlier leaders and was committed to increasing the democratization of the ROK society.

Roh loyally supported his predecessor Kim's Sunshine Policy, which Roh referred to as the Peace and Prosperity Policy. Roh moved forward in cooperative relations with the DPRK. A significant engagement was backed with South Korean investment. It was the Kaesong Industrial Zone (KIZ).

> The idea of the KIZ is based on the increasingly common assumption that the interests of both Koreas can be served by a combination of Southern capital and technologies with Northern cheap labor. So, it was decided to develop an industrial park in the vicinity of the DMZ. In this industrial park South Korean companies would employ North Korean workers who, laboring under the supervision of South Korean managers, would produce cheap items for sale in South Korea and overseas (Lankov, pp. 167-168).

This effort, a relatively modest operation in the beginning, was participated in by small- to medium-sized South Korean corporations, and was backed with governmental and corporate financing with leadership from the Roh administration. Increasingly, Roh's desire to seek accommodation with the North was backed by generous commitments from the ROK government.

> The DPRK received several major infrastructure projects in the North, including ROK financial commitments to enlarge the Kaesong Industrial Complex beyond the pilot phase, to build a railway connecting Kaesong to Sinuiju up the length of the northern portion of the peninsula, to build a highway connecting Kaesong in Pyongyang, and to build a port complex at Nampo ... [Roh] believed in the Sunshine Policy as the best way to deal with North Korea, and believed the policy was in South Korean national interests (Cha, p. 392).

The operations continued with substantial success in years beyond the end of the Roh presidency.

[B]y late 2010, some 120 South Korean companies operated in the KIZ, with 47,000 North Korean workers employed. Over half of the companies (71, to be exact) dealt with clothing and textiles. In 2010 the KIZ-based companies produced goods worth $323.3 million (again, slightly over half consisted of textiles and clothing). For the mammoth South Korean economy this is small change, but for the North this income is significant enough ... Indeed, the KIZ is a major cash cow for the North Korean state, providing an estimated annual revenue of $25-40 million. This allowed the numerous critics of the project to describe it as a 'slave labor camp.' The description is grossly unfair: even after the deductions, the KIZ jobs are by far the best-paid regular jobs in North Korea, so the locals strive hard to be accepted to a KIZ-based factory (Lankov, pp. 168-169).

That policy support for the North put Roh at odds with the Bush administration's deep skepticism about the North and its pursuits. But Roh was hardly anti-American. In 2004, the ROK committed three thousand troops to support American forces in Iraq. In 2007, Roh agreed to the Korea-US Free Trade Agreement that the Bush administration pushed for vigorously. That agreement was not adopted by the US Congress until 2011.

By 2006, Roh's generosity to the North and a coincident decline in the ROK economy eroded Roh's political support at home. Despite reaching out to the North, the DPRK continued to work on its nuclear weapons development. In 2006, the DPRK publicly tested intermediate-range missiles in July and exploded its first nuclear device in October. Small though the detonation was, the reality of the DPRK's nuclear weapons and missiles to deliver them was evident to the ROK, the US, and neighboring powers China, Japan, and Russia. Roh did not give up his hopes for accommodation with the DPRK. In October 2007, only a few months before his term of office would end, Roh spent two days in talks in Pyongyang that brought no tangible results. At home, the slumping economy was especially relevant to young people. "Because of Mr. Roh's inattentiveness to the economy, his approval rating first dipped below 30 percent two years ago [2004] as he lost most of his moderate supporters ... It fell further, into the teens this year, as his young backers also grew increasingly displeased about the economy and the high youth joblessness rate" (Onishi, *New York Times*, November 27, 2006).

In December 2007, the South Korean electorate chose Lee Myung-bak as its president, despite a vote total that was less than a majority (49 percent). His popular support far outdistanced Roh's favored candidate, Chung Dong-young, who got only 26 percent of the vote. Lee led the return of the Grand National Party to power after ten years of more liberal rule. Lee pledged to generate a domestic economic recovery, putting that ahead of reconciliation efforts regarding the DPRK. Moreover, he worked actively to achieve healthier South Korea-US relations. Even a former ROK ambassador to the US from the Roh administration credited the Lee government for its ability to restore the trust between the US and the ROK that had been lost during Roh's presidency (Onishi, *New York Times*, December 20, 2007).

Upon being established in the presidency, Lee assumed a harsher stance toward the DPRK than Roh's. At that time, the matter of nuclear arms in North Korea became more complex on the world scene because nuclear weaponization in Iran also became a controversial international issue. In 2009, the concern about nuclear arms in Iran received greater attention for a time than the DPRK situation, but both countries were considered to be an international threat to world peace by the US and other major powers: France, Russia, Germany, Britain, China, and Japan. The mix of nations could not come to terms on consistent sanctions to impose on these two countries. Nevertheless, Lee, directly concerned about the Korean Peninsula, proposed his own grand bargain: a package of economic incentives to the DPRK in return for it dismantling its nuclear weapons program. The details were to be worked out in a six-nation negotiation: besides the two Koreas, the negotiators would include China, Russia, the US, and Japan.

North Korea's desperate need for economic aid and food supply brought about lower level contacts between the two Koreas in 2008 and 2009. There were old issues, even talk about returning surviving ROK prisoners of war who had been held in the North for more than half a century. In January 2009, Lee sent a negotiator to the DPRK, offering to literally buy the old fuel rods from the Yongbyon nuclear reactor—in effect, pay a ransom to the North to unload its potential nuclear weapon raw material. The DPRK set an outlandishly high price and Lee rejected it. After that, President Lee was reluctant about a summit and, if held, it had to be in the South. "The North Koreans were outraged at what they saw as a reversal in Seoul's approach to the idea of a summit" (Oberdorfer and Carlin, p. 444). Not long thereafter, there were naval skirmishes near the boundary line on the Yellow Sea, in which South prevailed. The North responded in March 2010 by blowing up a South Korean patrol corvette, the *Cheonan,* killing forty-six South Korean sailors. "South Korean intelligence leaked to newspapers [in the ROK] that Kim and his son gave medals to the submarine unit responsible for the attack" (Cha, p. 103). After that, Lee was in no mood after that for deal making with the DPRK.

> Ultimately, the key determinant of Seoul's policy toward Pyongyang during Lee's administration was the degree of reciprocity that the North demonstrated. If the DPRK showed even a little interest in cooperating on denuclearization or on human rights, the Lee government reciprocated with a more conciliatory tone ... [Lee said] he would invite the DPRK leader to the 2012 Nuclear Summit in Seoul, but only if he undertook denuclearization. (The North Koreans subsequently rejected the invitation.) The irony of this is that while Lee's

standoffish attitude created considerable tension with the North and caused Pyongyang to eviscerate the South Korean leader in its propaganda, Lee Myung-bak arguably was the ROK President that Kim [Jong Il] wanted to establish contact with (Cha, p. 406). Lee believed that the DPRK needed the ROK's help for its own survival, so he took the stance of a hard bargainer. Not willing to meet Lee's terms, the DPRK resisted Lee's proposals for cooperation and instead responded with military attacks. "He [Lee] believed these attacks were out of desperation, given the [DPRK] regime's terrible state. He believed the DPRK was on its last legs, and was losing legitimacy among its people" (Cha, p. 407).

Interesting opinion data from North Koreans sheds some light on Lee's reading of the DPRK. The following results were reported in 2010 about the decline of regard for the *juche* ideology and for Kim Jong Il's leadership.

In 1994, around 80 percent of North Korean citizens stated a belief in the official [*juche*] ideology. However, this figure fell to around 64 percent in 2008 and 54.9 percent in 2009, of whom 26 percent expressed 'strong pride' and 29 percent 'some pride.' 42.7 percent expressed 'no pride for *juche* ideology,' constituting 32 percent of respondents who had 'not much pride' and 11 percent who had 'no pride at all.

Kim Jong-Il has been losing popularity throughout the past 10 years. According to a 1998 survey of 1694 North Korean refugees in China, only 8 percent expressed criticism of the Kim Jong Il leadership. However, negative sentiment toward his leadership has increased to 26.1 percent in 2008 and then 28.1 percent in 2009. It seems likely that Kim Jong Il can currently command the support of around or slightly less than 50 percent of the North Korean population (Park and Kim, pp. 127-128).

In the presidential campaign of 2012, South Koreans initially had three candidates to consider. An ally and former chief of staff to former President Roh, Moon Jae-in was the nominee of the left's Democratic United Party. He pledged to narrow income inequality and to reverse the Lee administration's hard-edged bargaining the North. "He has vowed to reverse President Lee's policy of linking economic assistance to progress in talks on ending North Korea's nuclear weapons program. Like other liberals, he sees economic cooperation essential to reconciliation and eventual inter-Korean reunification. He is eager to hold a summit meeting with the North's [new] leader, Kim Jong-un" (Choe, *New York Times*, November 23, 2012).

A wildcard candidate was Ahn Cheol-soo, a millionaire independent candidate who initially seemed to be a favorite of young voters. He criticized the existing parties, the dominance of the chaebols, and the inequality of income among the people. Although widely favored in early opinion polls, Ahn's candidacy was brief and he withdrew in order to support Moon, lest the two candidates on the liberal side split popular support and bring about Park's election.

In the face of President Lee's declining popularity, Park Geun-hye became the candidate of the right. Park's unique heritage was as the daughter of Park Chung Hee, the authoritarian president who was assassinated in 1979. He and his accomplishments a generation earlier were still remembered favorably for the economic renaissance that came with his militaristic presidency. She actively revitalized her party with fresh National Assembly candidates and a new party name, the New Frontier Party. "New Frontier sought to consolidate its conservative base by highlighting the nuclear and missile threats from North Korea. It depicted its liberal opponents as trying to appease North Korea and undermine South Korea's alliance with United States by demanding the renegotiation – and even the abrogation – of the trade deal with Washington" (Choe, *New York Times*, April 11, 2012).

While preparing for her election campaign for the presidency of South Korea, Ms. Park expressed her willingness to cultivate more, stronger relations with China. This message was explicitly expressed by Ms. Park to an international audience by means of a published article in *Foreign Affairs*. Her strategy was to gain leverage with China in order to manage the difficult relationships between ROK and the DPRK.

Because South Korea maintains both a critical alliance with the United States and a strategic partnership with China, confidence building on the Korean Peninsula would also improve trust between Beijing and Washington, creating a virtuous cycle in which a more cooperative U.S.-Chinese relationship would bolster more positive inter-Korean relations and vice versa. Although North Korea continues to depend heavily on China's economic and diplomatic protection, China's growing global stature and interest in improving its ties with the United States may limit its support for North Korea if Pyongyang continues to threaten the region's stability. North Korea may finally join the family of nations if it realizes that assistance from China cannot last forever (Park, *Foreign Affairs*, September 2011).

The 2012 election was close, but Ms. Park prevailed with 52 percent of the vote compared to Moon's 38 percent. From the *New York Times'* observer's vantage point, the election meant:

In the end, South Koreans appeared to prefer Ms. Park's calls to overhaul the chaebol over time to the more aggressive approach suggested by her rival, Mr. Moon. Indeed, what appeared to separate the two candidates throughout the election was how far they would go in implementing change.

Mr. Moon campaigned on a return to the Sunshine Policy, a combination of investments and aid to the North. Although Ms. Park criticized the 'inflexible' hard-line policy of the incumbent, President Lee Myung-bak, for failing to tame North Korea, she prefers a cautious rapprochement. She said she would decouple humanitarian aid from politics and try to meet the new North Korean leader, Kim Jong-un. But she insisted, like Mr. Lee, that any large scale investments be conditional on progress in ending North Korea's nuclear weapons program (Choe, *New York Times*, December 19, 2012).

In victory, Park also had the political advantage in that her New Frontier Party had an absolute majority in the National Assembly.

Ms. Park actively engaged in relations with China since her election. The South Korean and Chinese Security Councils entered into dialogue in 2013, a trust building exercise. In June 2015, the two countries signed a free trade agreement, an important step for South Korea. China has become its largest trading partner. President Park has since been able to enlarge the range of issues for cooperative actions with China. An acute American observer noted:

> Seoul's casual reference to unification within its statement on Park's meetings in China. The document states that 'the two sides also had in-depth discussions on the issue of unification. The Korean side stressed that with the Korean Peninsula in its 70th year of division, peaceful unification was a pressing aim, the realization of which would also contribute to promoting peace and prosperity in the region.' The Chinese side said that 'it supported the peaceful unification of the Korean Peninsula by the Korean people.' This was, however, the first time that China has ever mentioned unification in a statement with South Korea, signaling that bilateral discussions between Seoul and Beijing on unification have entered new territory. Of course, gaining Chinese support for South Korean positions in a unification scenario is

not all that Park is after: she is also looking to build a trilateral dialogue among China, South Korea, and her key ally, the United States, about the peninsula's future (Cha, *Foreign Affairs*, October 8, 2015).

To the extent that South Korea's relations with China through trade create a stronger interdependency between the two nations, Park actually gained leverage in dealing with the DPRK that is so dependent upon China's sufferance and support.

It is relevant to briefly note the present strength of the South Korean economy. The Park administration launched a three-year economic innovation plan to achieve financial and regulatory reforms. The ROK's productivity continues to grow, despite some vagaries. After an economic setback in 2008-2009, the ROK's gross domestic product (GNP) has increased steadily. Its first trillion dollar GNP year was in 2007. In 2014, it reached $1.45 trillion. Its annual foreign trade volume has exceeded a trillion dollars each year since 2013 (*Facts About Korea*, 2015). Park's administration still has unsolved issues to deal with regarding employment, and it has evoked opposition from unions that has taken the form of militant labor activism. However, the dominant issues currently include the provocations that come from the ROK's obstreperous neighbor, the DPRK.

CHAPTER 6: NORTH KOREA: CULTURE AND LIFE

A helpful starting point for this chapter is a recent country report from the US Central Intelligence Agency. It offers a rather grim overview of the economy that shapes the living conditions in the DPRK. The key words and phrases in the description include "economic problems," "persistent shortages," "severe famine," "prolonged malnutrition," "inflation," "dilapidated rail network," and "firm political control remains the government's overriding concern."

Economy - overview:

North Korea, one of the world's most centrally directed and least open economies, faces chronic economic problems. Industrial capital stock is nearly beyond repair as a result of years of under-investment, shortages of spare parts, and poor maintenance. Large-scale military spending draws off resources needed for investment and civilian consumption. Industrial and power outputs have stagnated for years at a fraction of pre-1990 levels. Frequent weather-related crop failures aggravated chronic food shortages caused by on-going systemic problems, including a lack of arable land, collective farming practices, poor soil quality, insufficient fertilization, and persistent shortages of tractors and fuel.

The mid-1990s were marked by severe famine and widespread starvation. Significant food aid was provided by the international community through 2009. Since that time, food assistance has declined significantly. In the last few years, domestic corn and rice production has been somewhat better, although domestic production does not fully satisfy demand. A large portion of the population continues to suffer from prolonged malnutrition and poor living conditions. Since 2002, the government has allowed informal markets to begin selling a wider range of goods. It also implemented changes in the management process of communal farms in an effort to boost agricultural output.

In December 2009, North Korea carried out a redenomination of its currency, capping the amount of North Korean won that could be exchanged for the new notes, and limiting the exchange to a one-week window. A concurrent crackdown on markets and foreign currency use yielded severe shortages and inflation, forcing Pyongyang to ease the restrictions by February 2010. In response to the sinking of the South Korean warship Cheonan and the shelling of Yeonpyeong Island in 2010, South Korea's government cut off most aid, trade, and bilateral cooperation activities, with the exception of operations at the Kaesong Industrial Complex. North Korea continued efforts to develop special economic zones and expressed willingness to permit construction of a trilateral gas pipeline that would carry Russian natural gas to South Korea. North Korea is also working with Russia to refurbish North Korea's dilapidated rail network and jointly rebuilt a link between a North Korean port in the Rason Special Economic Zone and the Russian rail network.

The North Korean government continues to stress

its goal of improving the overall standard of living, but has taken few steps to make that goal a reality for its populace. In 2013-2014, the regime rolled out 20 new economic development zones - now totaling 25 - set up for foreign investors, although the initiative remains in its infancy. Firm political control remains the government's overriding concern, which likely will inhibit changes to North Korea's current economic system.

www.cia.gov/library/publications/the-world-factbook/geos/kn.html, accessed 2/18.16.

Although contemporary news stories focus upon Kim Jong Un and North Korea's leaders and its continuing adventurism with nuclear weapons and long-range missiles, the attention in this discussion examines what has been going on within the DPRK as it affects the culture and lives of the ordinary people. Westerners are likely to imagine that the socialist nature of the North Korean society would provide for substantial equality among the citizenry. That is not the case. In North Korea, there is an elaborate caste system understood as *songbun*. There are three primary distinctions that differentiate the political reliability of the people according to the background and history of each person's family. One's permanent placement has significant consequences for a person's work assignment, education, place of residence, provision of services, and quality of housing.

At the bottom of the three-tiered system was the so-called hostile class. These included families who had been rich peasants or whose family origins hailed from South Korea or Japan. People of this rank were closely watched by neighborhood organizations called *inminban*, literally 'people's group,' whose members reported anything suspicious. The second tier, the so-called wavering class, hailed from families of middle-class peasants, traders or owners of small businesses. The upper class, the core [or loyal] class, was composed of people whose families had traditionally been workers, soldiers, or party members. Only members of the core class, which constituted roughly 15 percent of the population, were able to live in Pyongyang, considered a privilege. By contrast, members of the hostile class were relocated to remote regions of the country beginning in the late 1950s, especially the northeast where most of North Korea's mines and infamous concentration camps were located. This stratified classification system would later have important implications for the famine, as it was precisely these parts of the country that experienced the severest deprivations (Jager, p. 453).

The implications of this intentionally discriminatory system of citizen identification show in the choices people make in marriage. Rarely do individuals marry persons of the rank below themselves. They typically choose partners of like social rank. Rank has always been of significant consequence in regard to food supply. Food availability in North Korea has been managed with the government's Primary Distribution System (PDS). In effect, the necessities of life are distributed as compensation for employment. However, stratification assures that the ranking officials, military personnel, and essential laborers receive the most and best food. Those in the hostile class, less educated, and less well-placed in employment have to do with less, and especially much less when food is scarce.

During the 1990s, a variety of factors brought about severe famine in the DPRK. According to the *New York Times*, "during the great famine of the 1990s, between 600,000 and 2.5 million people died of hunger" (Stanton and Lee, March 17, 2014). That wide range of estimates is because the DPRK does not produce accurate reports, and estimates by outsiders vary. A more careful analysis provides this report: "estimates put excess mortality as a result of the food crisis at between 600,000 and 1,000,000; 3 to 5 percent of the total North Korean population" (Cha, p. 188).

The famine was largely because of a decline and failure of North Korean agriculture. Food production until the 1990s was apparently adequate.

> Then the situation began to deteriorate. Deprived of fuel, electricity, and fertilizer and manned by workers who had little incentive to care about the future harvest, the system collapsed. The 1996 harvest was a mere 2.5-2.8 million metric tons -- half of what would have been enough to keep the population fed ... From 1993 to 1994, rations were increasingly delayed and/or delivered only partially. The delays began in more remote areas of the countryside, but soon spread to major cities. After the floods, the PDS rations almost completely stopped (Lankov, pp. 78-79).

When the capability of the PDS failed, it left the masses struggling for survival. "Outside of Pyongyang, only party cadres, police personnel, military officials, and the workers at military factories continued to receive their rations, and even those privileged groups did not necessarily receive full allowances in the years between 1996 and 2000" (Lankov, p. 79).

There are a few exit options for North Koreans who want to leave the country, whether there is a food crisis or not. The DPRK census of 2008 accounts for a population of twenty-four million people but it does not report outmigration. Movement over the armed border at the 38th parallel is well-nigh impossible. The most prominent exit is on the northern border into China. However, since 1986, the official policy of the People's Republic of China is to protect the border and return any refugees who might have managed across it. Nevertheless, the level of enforcement varies and, as the stories from refugees reveal, bribery is commonplace. "Numbers are hard to come by, since no organization is allowed to conduct a systematic survey. The Chinese official estimate is about 10,000. But activists, press and other governments put the number as high as 100,000 to 300,000" (Cha, p. 178). Another report states that "between 1998 and 1999, when the famine was at its height, it was estimated that anywhere from 150,000 and 195,000 North Koreans were hiding in China. After 2005 the numbers shrank dramatically, but it is estimated that at any given moment there are still between 20,000 and 40,000 North Korean refugees hiding in China" (Lankov, p. 94).

A hugely difficult option for North Korean refugees is to find passage to South Korea. As of 2000, the estimated number of North Korean refugees in the ROK was only 1,100; but by 2012, the number had increased to an estimated 23,000 (Lankov, p. 96). During the 1980s, when defections from North Korea to the ROK were uncommon, South Koreans were highly welcoming. Indeed, refugees who reached a South Korean embassy were helped with safe transportation to Seoul. But increasingly during the 1990s and since, the ROK became less welcoming. Refugees are turned away at South Korean embassies and consulates. Moreover, many North Korean refugees who have entered the South have not adapted very well to the fast-paced life of contemporary South Korea, where educational accomplishment is high, and work place technology is modern and complex. Refugees do not find full-time employment easily and the jobs they fill are low-skill and mostly menial. Although there are organizations to assist refugees, increasingly they are thought of as a potential burden to the South Korean government. It appears South Korea is content to tolerate a small contingent of North Korean ex-patriots, but prefers for them to remain unobtrusive and a minimal burden on public services. Defectors were applauded and coddled as propaganda victories over the North when they came during the 1980s, but more recently, North Korean-refugee status is not a significantly rewarded one.

There is a useful way to get a close-up of North Korea. A number of useful biographies and journalistic reports have been published about life in North Korea. Don Oberdorfer, a *Washington Post* journalist, received what was at the time a rare look at Pyongyang in 1991. The city was leveled during the Korean War. "Kim Il Sung had rebuilt it from the

ashes to a meticulously planned urban center of broad bou-
levards, monumental structures, and square-cut apartment
buildings that resembled a stage set more than a working
capital. Indeed, it was a synthetic city in many respects:
according to foreign diplomats, the population was periodi-
cally screened, and the sick, elderly, or disabled, along with
anyone deemed politically unreliable, were evicted from
the capital" (Oberdorfer and Carlin, pp. 183-184). Visiting
outsiders were shown the Tower of the *Juche* Idea, built
to commemorate Kim Il Sung's self-reliance ideology, the
Arch of Triumph (mentioned before), and the Kim Il Sung
Stadium that seats a hundred thousand people for occasional massive celebrations.

More illuminating descriptions of typical life come from
stories by North Korean refugees. Several have been published and reveal their painful lives in the North and the
difficulties they experienced to enter South Korea. I have
selected passages from the stories of three refugees.

Kang Chol-hwan is a Korean whose family returned to North
Korea after a refugee experience in Japan. An estimated
one hundred thousand ethnic Koreans were repatriated
from Japan in the early 1960s, referred to as the "Great
Movement of the Korean People." Initially, Kang's family
was part of the "loyal" class. However, because these
Koreans came with wealth and goods, benefits of Japan's
flourishing capitalism, many were assigned to the "wavering class." With that came close scrutiny about devotion
to North Korean ideology and faithfulness to the regime.
For the Kang family, the Japanese connection caused
suspicions regarding Kang's grandfather. In time, the Kim
regime put Kang's family into the "hostile" class, and even
forced them into a camp for "reeducation." Eventually,
Kang regained entrance back into North Korean society.
However, it was a life under surveillance. He feared that a
minor violation, particularly listening to South Korean radio
broadcasts, would cause him to be labeled a recidivist. He
would then be sent back to the restrictions of camp life.

Kang successfully took flight. Here are excerpts from his story.

Kang Chol-hwan and Pierre Rigoulot, translated by Yair Reiner. *The Aquariums of Pyongyang: Ten Years in the North Korean Gulag.* New York Basic Books Edition, 2005. Originally published in French in 2000.

To my childish eyes and to those of all my friends, Kim Il Sung and Kim Jong Il were perfect beings, untarnished by any base human function. I was convinced, as we all were, that neither of them urinated or defecated. Who could imagine such things of gods? In the portraits of their paternal faces I found comfort and all that was protecting, kindly, self-assured (p. 3).

Like everyone in my [school] class, I signed up for the Pupils' Red Army. What a sight we must have made marching into battle, fake machine guns slung across our shoulders. Though we mostly just learned to form ranks and sing while marching, we loved these exercises and never had to be asked twice to strike a military pose. Right away we felt like we were Kim Il Sung's little soldiers. We were never asked to do anything too demanding. The training was adapted to our tender age and generally consisted of marching around the schoolyard a few times or around a block of houses (p. 5).

My family enjoyed a level of comfort foreign to most North Korean homes, even in Pyongyang. We had a refrigerator, washing machine, vacuum cleaner, and even the most sought-after of all luxury goods: a color television set, on which, to our great delight, we could watch the dramatic political-crime series 'Clean Hands.' Even our clothes seemed rich compared to those of our neighbors, to whom my grandmother would often give away what we no longer needed (p. 6).

Koreans [living in Japan during and after WW II] never had an easy time integrating into Japanese life and often were targets of prejudice. The North Korean propaganda [to lure Koreans in Japan] thus resonated with many in the diaspora, and thousands responded to Kim Il Sung's call to return. Well-to-do Koreans such as my grandparents could expect to be wooed with an equal measure of ideological arguments and fantastical promises: there were managerial positions awaiting them, they were entitled to a beautiful home, they would have no material worries, and their children would be able to study in Moscow. Grandfather was rather against the idea, Grandmother all for it. Interminable conversations followed, from which my grandmother ultimately emerged victorious. No one was particularly surprised. And so it was that the family found itself heading North Korea (p. 19).

[In time] my grandfather's position [became] the cause of constant worry, and it eventually cost him his life. He was a businessman who had learned how to get things done under a free market system [in Japan]. When faced with the model of North Korean bureaucracy, he tended to let his frustration show, which in retrospect was not wise. Though he only ever criticized the country's excellent political and economic methods 'for the sake of improving and strengthening the country,' ... He refused to keep quiet ... Despite all the honors and benefits that sprang from my grandparents' positions, North Korean life was not meeting the family's expectations ... I think Grandfather first to realize he'd been had ... It was in July 1977. One night he didn't come home from work. The police said they knew nothing" (pp. 29, 30, 36).

A few weeks later, "I remember perfectly the moment I first heard pronounced the name of Yodok. One of the [security] agents had begun rifling through my mother's lingerie, and seeing her private things tossed across the room, my mother allowed her voice to rise. Outraged, the man with the notebook jumped to his feet, ordering her to shut up, then pulled out a paper from which he read out loud. According to the document, my grandfather had committed 'a crime of high treason,' the consequence of which was that his family — all of us there gathered, that is — was 'immediately' to present itself at the secure zone in Yodok, a canton of which I had never heard (p. 39).

In Yoduk, "The collection of 10 huts that made up our immediate surroundings constituted what we prisoners called a 'village' ...Each village consolidated a specific category of detainees. Ours, which was built in 1974, was inhabited solely by former Japanese residents and their families. The segregation served as tacit recognition of our difficult integration into North Korean society as well as a way of isolating all mention of the capitalist hell existing outside the country's borders. For the same reason we were also forbidden — under threat of severe punishment — from having any contact with prisoners from other villages (pp. 52- 53).

In all my time in Yoduk, I only received uniforms twice, and though they quickly came apart, they were all I had to wear — day after day, year after year, in field, mine, forest, and mountain. During our years of detention, rags were often the only clothing we had.... We were also constantly on the lookout for ways to steal more clothes. Working on a funeral crew, we never buried a corpse without first stripping it naked (p. 61-62).

After a decade in Yoduk, my knowledge of the camp boils down to this: of Yoduk's ten villages, four were for redeemables and six were for irredeemables, or political criminals. The latter group lived in a high-security zone that was separated from ours by several hills, as well as by rows of barbed wire rolled out along the valley's floor. The irredeemables were all lifers. They knew they were never leaving the camp ... In my part of the camp, the detainees still held to the hope of getting out one day. They set their teeth, suffered in silence, tried to hold out. Hope clung to their bodies even when it seemed to abandon their minds. But those in the high security zone harbored no hope of returning to normal life (p. 80).

As the years passed, another feeling began to disturb my daily existence: the feeling of injustice, which grew sharper when I considered the discrepancy between everything I had been taught and all that I was living ... I had memorized almost entirely *A Letter to New Korea's Much Beloved Children*, which Kim Il Sung wrote for the occasion of the Day of Children, 'who are the treasure of our country and its future' ... And yet I was being made to pay for my grandfather's crimes. I was no longer the jewel in Kim Il Sung's eye. I was a prisoner: filthy, tattered, hungry, spent. All those beautiful words had been flouted with perfect impunity (p. 153).

And then one day the nightmare was over ... On February 16, 1987, all the prisoners in the village were summoned to the large meeting hall for the chance to celebrate the birth and sing the praises of Kim Jong Il. The camp's security chief, wearing his full dress uniform, gave a speech about the benevolence of our Dear Leader ... The security chief then announced that some of us were going to be released ... I heard my family's name being called! ...The head of the camp then explained that President Kim Il Sung and his son, our dear leader Kim Jong Il, had decided that, given the ideological progress demonstrated by the aforementioned prisoners, an opportunity would be given them to work for the fatherland outside the confines of Yodok. The remaining prisoners should let this gesture stand as proof of our leaders' boundless solicitude ... [M]y family was soon moved to a small town near the district's industrial center. We lived there from 1987 to 1990, exchanging exhausting agricultural work for less taxing jobs in shops and factories (pp. 155-157, 164).

I told my family I would be going away for a few days and, on the eve of my departure, informed my girlfriend that I wouldn't see her for a while because of work ... I nearly burst into tears. I had lie to her, I was leaving, and she thought I was coming back. It was unbearable. I'm sure she hated leaving the way I did, but there was the other way ... We crossed the Yalu River on foot. Once on the Chinese side, it only took a few minutes to reach the house of the man we hoped would eventually lead us out of the dangerous border zone ... He was a young man, between twenty-two and twenty-five years old, a Chinese citizen of Korean ancestry who made his living by cross-border trading, importing deer antlers and ginseng from North Korea and exporting socks, sweaters, and scarves back across. It was a profitable business, because Chinese goods are expensive in the North (pp. 193, 195).

Our departure [by merchant ship from Dalian] was set for September 14 [1992]. The captain planned everything in great detail, because carrying it out wouldn't be easy ... At one point the ship stopped for several hours. I imagine it was awaiting word from Seoul about how to proceed. If so, the orders finally came and, three hours later, as night was falling, we arrived at the military port of Inchon, not far from Seoul ... I [was] given long interrogations

... [A security agent] handed me a sheet of paper and asked me to draw a map of Yodok. I did as I was told, trying to remember every detail and devoting particular attention to Ipsok, the executions site, and to the mountains ... He was beginning to trust me. I then identified the other structures for him: the bachelor's [sic] barracks, the distillery ... This went on for quite a while. I told him everything I knew. The atmosphere in the room changed completely since the start of the questioning. The agent was relaxed, his forced geniality had turned to genuine good humor, and I confided in him with perfect trust. The debriefing lasted a week (pp. 217, 220-221).

After six months of continuous chaperoning, I was allowed to rent an apartment, and a local policeman was assigned to my case ... After two years, I was allowed to live entirely on my own. The security agents' presence had been generally more helpful than burdensome ... More important, [they] taught me how to face hardships in my new world (p. 226).

Reunification is inevitable, but it can only take place once Pyongyang has stopped crucifying the population under its control. How can we stand by while troops of orphans cross the Yalu and the Tumen rivers seeking refuge in China? How can we stand by while parents sell their daughters for something to eat? I don't want to see any more skeletal children with wide, frightened eyes. I don't want any more children sent to the camps and their mothers forced to divorce their fathers. I want their grandfathers to be around to tell them stories – and their giggles on the banks of the Daedong never to be interrupted by the arrival of bureaucrats from the Security Force (pp. 237-238).

Shin Dong-hyuk's life story was unraveled by Blaine Harden. Kang, whose family sank from the loyal class to be in the hostile class of society, was one nevertheless of the "redeemables." Shin, however, was born in prison to a couple of irredeemables. Shin grew to manhood in Camp 14, escaping on January 2, 2005. Like Kang, he made his way into China, eventually arriving in Shanghai. In February 2006, with help from a South Korean journalist, he was brought into and assisted by the South Korean consulate. His unique story of imprisonment and escape so interested the South Korean National Intelligence Service that he was brought to Seoul and eventually received South Korean citizenship. This is a small part of his story.

Harden, Blaine. Escape from Camp 14: One Man's Remarkable Odyssey. New York: Penguin books, 2013

Nine years after his mother's hanging, Shin squirmed through an electric fence and ran off through the snow. It was January 2, 2005. Before then, no one born in a North Korean political prisoner camp had ever escaped. As far as can be determined Shin is still the only one to do it ... His name is now Shin Dong- hyuk. He changed it after arriving in South Korea, an attempt to reinvent himself as a free man. He is handsome, with quick, wary eyes (p. 1).

Shin was born a slave and raised behind a high-voltage barbed wire fence. He was educated in a camp school to read and count at a rudimentary level. Because his blood was tainted by the perceived crimes of his father's brothers, he lived below the law. For him, nothing was possible. His state-prescribed career trajectory was hard labor and an early death from disease brought on by chronic hunger – all without any charge or a trial or an appeal, and all in secrecy ... His mother beat him, and he viewed her as a competitor for food. His father, who was allowed by guards to sleep with his mother just five nights a year, ignored him. His brother was a stranger. Children in the camp were untrustworthy and abusive. Before he learned anything else, Shin learned to survive by snitching on all of them. Love and mercy and family were words without meaning. God did not appear or die. Shin had never heard of him ... Unlike those who have survived a concentration camp, Shin had not been torn away from a civilized existence and forced to descend into hell. He was born and raised there. He accepted its values. He called it home (pp.2-4).

Shin's camp, number 14, is a complete control district. By reputation it is the toughest of them all because of its particularly brutal working conditions, the vigilance of its guards, and the state's unforgiving view of the seriousness of the crimes committed by its inmates, many of whom are purged officials from the ruling party, the government, and the military, along with their families. Established in 1959 in central Korea North Korea – Kaechon, South Pyongan Province – Camp 14 holds an estimated fifteen thousand prisoners. About thirty miles long and fifty miles wide, it has farms, mines, and factories threaded through steep mountain valleys (p.5).

A reward marriage was the only safe way around the no-sex rule. Marriage was dangled in front of prisoners as the ultimate bonus for hard work and reliable snitching ... Shin's father, Shin Gyung Sub, told Shin that guards gave him Jang [his mother] as payment for his skill in operating a metal lathe in the camp's machine shop. Shin's mother never told Shin why she had been given the honor of marriage ... After their marriage, the couple was allowed sleep together for five consecutive nights. From then on, Shin's father, who continued to live in a dormitory at his worksite, was permitted to visit Jang a few times a year. Their liaison produced two sons. The eldest, He Geun, was born in 1974. Shin was born eight years later (pp.17-18).

The unforgivable crime Shin's father had committed was being the brother of two young men who fled south during a fratricidal war that razed much of the Korean Peninsula and divided hundreds of thousands of families. Shin's unforgivable crime was being his father's son. Shin's father had never explained any of this (p.57).

When Shin was thirteen years old, his mother and brother tried to escape the camp. Shin informed the security guards of their plans and they were caught. Nevertheless, Shin was imprisoned and initially treated as if he were an accomplice. After physical punishment and imprisonment, he was exonerated but then forced to witness the execution of his mother and brother. It was not until 2004 that Shin made plans to attempt escape with Park, one of his co-workers. The attempt, necessitating a getaway through an electrified fence, was made on January 2, 2005.

Their plan had been for Shin to stay in the lead until they got clear of the fence, but he slipped and fell to his knees on the icy patrol trail. Park [Shin's older companion, a political prisoner] was first to the fence. Falling on his knees, he shoved his arms, head, and shoulders between the two lowest strands of wire. Seconds later, Shin saw sparks and smelled burning flesh ... Before Shin could get to his feet, Park had stopped moving. He may already have been dead. The weight of his body pulled down the bottom strand of wire, pinning it against the snowy ground and creating a small gap in the fence. Without hesitation, Shin crawled over his friend's body, using it as a kind of insulating pad.... Shin's success in crawling through an electric fence designed to kill seems to have been a function of luck. His was astoundingly good; Park's was terrible ... When he cleared the fence, he had no idea where to go. At the crest of the mountain, the only direction he could comprehend was down (pp, 117-119).

Racing downhill in early evening darkness through cornfield stubble, Shin came across a farmer's shed half buried in the hillside ... Helped by moonlight, he searched the shed for something else to eat. Instead he spotted an old pair of cotton shoes and a worn military uniform ... He put on the ratty, too-big uniform and slipped his feet into the cotton shoes. No longer instantly recognizable as a runaway prisoner, he had become just another ill-clothed, ill-shod, and ill-nourished North Korean ... He felt wonderfully free – and, as best he could determine, no one was looking for him (pp. 120-121 and 123).

When Shin was stuck in Gilju in January 2005, the food situation was much less dire ... By himself, he went around to the back of a vacant house and broke in through a window. Inside, he found winter clothes, a military-style woolen hat, and a fifteen pound bag of rice. He changed into the warmer clothes and carried the rice in his backpack to a Gilju merchant, who bought it for six thousand wan, about six dollars. With a new wad of cash for food and bribes ... Shin walked to the freight yard at Gilju station and crawled aboard a northbound boxcar [heading for China] (pp. 138-139).

Shin could not have escaped North Korea without an abundance of luck, especially at the border. As he bribed his way toward China in late January 2005, a window happened to be open, allowing relatively low-risk illegal passage across the border ... In late 2005, with winter rolling into the mountains, Shin decided to make his move. He had heard on the radio that Korean churches in China sometimes helped defectors. So he came up with a sketchy plan: he would travel west and south, putting as much distance as possible between himself, North Korea, and the border patrol soldiers. Then he would seek out friendly Koreans.

With their help, he hoped to find a stable job in southern China and build a low-profile life (pp. 142, 155-156).

Making his way cautiously across the Chinese countryside, Shin managed to get to Shanghai. There, Shin coincidentally met a South Korean journalist who learned from Shin about his North Korean identity and personal history. The journalist accompanied Shin to the South Korean Consulate in Shanghai. There, he told his story to South Korean officials, who were helpful.

Then, after six months inside the consulate, Shin flew to Seoul where the South Korean National Intelligence Service took an uncommon interest in him. During interrogation that lasted about two weeks, Shin told NIS agents his life story ... During his first month at Hanawon, he received documents and photo identification that certified his South Korea citizenship, which the government automatically bestows on all those who flee the North (pp. 161 and 163).

As word spread in Seoul of his birth in and escape from a no-exit labor camp, he began to meet many of the South's leading human rights activists and heads of defector organizations. His story was vetted and scrutinized by former prisoners and guards from the camps as well as by human rights lawyers, South Korean journalists, and other experts with extensive knowledge of the camps. His understanding of how the camps operate, his scarred body, and the haunted look in his eyes were persuasive – and he was widely acknowledged as the first North Korean to come south after escaping from a political prison (p. 168).

'It is just a matter of time,' Shin told me, before North Korea decides to destroy the camps. 'I hope that the United States, through pressure and persuasion, can convince [the North Korean government] not to murder all those people in the camps.' Shin had not figured out how to pay his bills, make a good living, or find a girlfriend in South Korea. But he had decided what he wanted to do with the rest of his life: he would be a human rights activist and raise international awareness about the existence of the labor camps ... In response to questions about his safety, Shin was unfazed. He was not afraid. He said he would never stop talking about what happened to him inside Camp 14 until the North Korean gulag was shut down and all its prisoners were set free (pp. 177 and 197).

A third story of escape is from a young woman, Eunsun Kim. The majority of North Korean refugees are women, so this escape is more typical than the stories above. Kim grew up in an ordinary way in a small North Korean town of Eundeok. Located in the northeastern part of the country, it is only fifteen kilometers from the Tumen River, on the border with China. Told in her own voice, her story opens during her childhood at the height of the famine in 1997. Her departure, with her mother and sister, took her on a nine year journey to freedom.

Eunsun Kim, with Sebastien Falletti, translated by David Tian. *A Thousand Miles to Freedom: My Escape from North Korea (New* York: St. Martin's Press, 2015)

December, 1997

For nearly a week, I had been alone in our tiny, freezing apartment in Eundeok, the town in North Korea where I was born. Other than a coffee table and a wooden dresser, my parents had sold all of our furniture to buy food to fill our stomachs. Even the carpeting was gone so I slept on the cement floor in a makeshift sleeping bag pulled together from old clothes. The walls were completely bare except for two framed, side-by-side portraits of our "Eternal President" Kim Il Sung and his successor, the "Dear Leader" Kim Jong Il, staring down at me. Selling these portraits would have been considered sacrilege, punishable by death.

Even though darkness was falling on this late December afternoon I could still manage to read what I was writing ... I was sure I was about to die of hunger. So I started to write my last will and testament. I was eleven years old. (pp. 1-2)

Since 1995, my family members had been slowly dying one after another, and the three of us [Eunsun, her sister Keumsun and her mother] were next on the list. Within a span of two years, my mother had lost my grandmother and then my grandfather shortly afterward. Just one month ago, it had been my father's turn to go. Behind her closed eyes, my mom must have been watching this seemingly endless nightmare replay over and over again in her mind (p. 39).

After escaping into China, Eunsun recounts being arrested by Chinese police and returned across the border to North Korea. She tells of a violent and abusive interrogation:

Then I was thrown into a cell where some sixty other women were already crammed like cattle. The cell was tiny and was hardly built to fit sixty people. On one side there were steel bars preventing us from escaping. On the other side, there was a simple hole in the ground where we could go to the bathroom, right in front of everyone. There wasn't enough space to lie down or stretch ... That night, for the first time in my life, I began to feel anger toward my country. Up until then, I'd never felt any hatred toward North Korea. We only left for China in order to survive, because we didn't have any food. We didn't have anything against Kim Jong II, nor did we have anything against the system – we were apolitical. But in that prison, for the first time, my eyes were opened to the horrors perpetuated by the Kim regime, and I felt my anger begin to build (pp. 112-113).

Having again escaped into China, Eunsun describes some of her teenage experiences:

> During the winter of 2002, six months after she left for the city, Keumsun asked me whether I wanted to come join her. She had found a job for me in a bakery in Won Chin, the city next to where she lived. I was 16, and I was nervous about leaving my mom for the first time, but I had to learn how to take care of myself so I accepted her offer ...
>
> Throughout the course of several months, I began to feel more and more comfortable at the bakery. But at the start of summer 2003, a new turn of events derailed the life I was building. One day, I was told to go to the counter in the bakery. There was a phone call for me. My heart started pounding in worry. 'I couldn't take it anymore. I left the farm. I couldn't stand that life anymore,' my mother informed me with a hint of guilt in her voice ...
>
> 'Let's go to Dalian. It's a large city and we'll have more opportunities to find work and less risk of getting arrested,' Keumsun said. I got into contact with my mom again, and we persuaded her to leave with us to head south, to Dalian [a port city on the Liaodong Peninsula, at the southern tip of China's northeastern Liaoning Province] It's the largest metropolis in the region, an entirely different environment waited for us there. I was hoping that this new environment would be a change for the better (pp. 129, 131, 134).

After another lengthy move and spending some time working in Shanghai, the three refugees were united once more:

> Little by little, I started to dream about going to South Korea. In Shanghai, thanks to the South

Koreans who treated us so nicely, I rediscovered my roots, my native language, and formed a clearer picture of the world. But I couldn't study, nor hope to find a good job, as long as I was here ill legally. I didn't want to be an illegal resident, or to live with fake identification, for the rest of my life. Here, we still lived in constant fear of getting arrested. In South Korea, I would finally be able to live my life in the open. Maybe I could even start going to school again. I learned that in South Korea, the government granted South Korean citizenship to all escapees from North Korea, as long as you could prove that you weren't a spy. The only issue was getting there (p. 144).

Keumsun found a Chinese mate in Shanghai, but Eunsun and her mother committed themselves to the hazardous prospect of getting to South Korea by way of Mongolia.

Mom and I had just traveled through half of China with our savings hidden in our clothing and with fear in our hearts. We had first reported the train toward Beijing, then got on a bus heading northwest toward the Mongolian border"(pp.149-150).

After three days of waiting [in Ulan Bator, Mongolia], I was called in for an interrogation with a South Korean official. I was nervous, but Mom was right there next to me. I responded carefully to all the questions. They wanted to know everything: where I was from, how I'd gotten here, whether the woman next to me was really my mother. These questions were justified; South Korea was always on the lookout for possible spies from the North who would try to infiltrate the south (pp.166-167).

After flying to South Korea, there was much more interrogation by South Korean officials.

Overall, my interrogations went fairly smoothly, especially since I later learned that some people were forced to take lie detector tests ... One day, however, the torment ended, and I was allowed to return to the living quarters to see my mom. Finally we could speak to each other. I began to understand that I had passed the final test (p. 177).

It seems absurd and ungrateful, but all of a sudden, after making it all the way to South Korea in obtaining the papers that we never imagine we'd receive, after the sheer joy of this day when we had finally and totally escaped from our life of hiding, after being welcomed in Houston this new country, I was overcome by an immense feeling of sadness. It was as if everything, all the burdens and hardships of the past nine years, came back to me at that moment. The future loomed ahead like unfamiliar territory we had to conquer. I was overwhelmed. Mom must have been feeling the same way (p. 185).

On April 15, 2012, the North Korean regime was preparing to celebrate Kim Il Sung's hundredth birthday, the birthday of the 'Eternal President.' North Korean propaganda had promised the population that the country would become a 'rich and powerful' nation by this time. Reading these headlines in the newspaper, I couldn't help but crack a smile, wavering between sadness and anger. When I was young, and when Kim Il Sung was still alive, he had promised us 'rice and beef soup' every day. However, more than twenty years later, this simple objective has still not been achieved. I am in a position to judge, because my grandparents and my father died from hunger. And so the promise of a 'rich and powerful' nation was a flat-out lie, despite the lavish celebrations orchestrated by the regime (p. 211).

It's my dream of one day seeing my people in the north free from a dictatorship that has kept them in fear, misery, and isolation from the rest of the world for decades. For this dream to become a reality, the whole world must open its eyes to the horrors currently taking place in North Korea. The Kim dynasty has so successfully isolated my country that it would be easy for the rest of the world to forget about us. If my memoir can play even a small part in raising global awareness about our suffering and about the tragedies taking place at the hands of this regime, then all that I have endured will not have been in vain (pp. 227-228).

One more dreary picture of North Korean life comes from Barbara Demick, author of *Nothing to Envy: Ordinary Lives in North Korea.* Demick was a *Los Angeles Times* correspondent stationed in Seoul in 2001. Her book is based upon seven years of conversations with approximately one hundred North Korean defectors, most living, at the time, either in South Korea or China. She made nine trips into North Korea between 2001 and 2008. Her images, recorded after her last visit in 2008, are detailed in the epilogue to her book, dated July 2010.

In September 2008, on an excursion through Nampo [a west coast harbor city about 25 miles from Pyongyang] … I saw people who appeared to be homeless sleeping on the grass along the main street. Others squatted on their haunches, heads down, apparently having nothing to do at 10 o'clock on a weekday morning. Walking barefoot along the sidewalk was a boy of about nine years old wearing a mud-stained uniform that hung below his knees. That was the first time I'd seen one of the notorious wanderings swallows, the *kochebi*. [Children whose parents had died or gone off to find food. Left to fend for themselves, they tended to flock like pigeons scavenging for crumbs at the train station. They were a strange migratory phenomenon in a country that previously had never heard of homelessness.]

There was evidence all along the twenty-five-mile drive between Pyongyang and Nampo of the extent to which North Korea's able-bodied population was enlisted in the production of food. Middle-aged office ladies were marched out to the countryside, carrying pocketbooks and with shovels slung over their shoulders. On the side of the road, older people sifted through the grass on their hands and knees in search of edible weeds. The countryside reeked of the night soil that is still used instead of chemical fertilizer. There were few motorized vehicles in the fields. Trucks belching smoke appeared to have been retrofitted to burn wood and corn cobs instead of gasoline. People carried huge sacks on their backs, hunched over as they walked along rusted railroad tracks that clearly hadn't been used in years (Demick, pp. 293-294).

It is a North Korean phenomenon that many have observed. For lack of chairs or benches, the people sit for hours on their haunches, along the sides of roads, in parks, in the market. They stare straight ahead as though they are waiting – for a tram, maybe, or a passing car, a friend or a relative. Maybe they are waiting for nothing in particular, just waiting for something to change (Demick, p. 296).

The divergence of the two Koreas from one another since their separate constitutions in 1948 is dramatic politically, economically, socially, and culturally. Everything about daily life in the DPRK reeks of regimen, deprivation, and hardship. The absence of freedom and individual fulfillment keeps even neighbors, co-workers, and family members from trusting one another. The great majority of the people, both collectively and individually, are deprived of opportunity and upward mobility. The means of communication are dedicated to the ruling regime's propaganda and control over the ordinary people. The sustenance that Kim Il Sung, the Great Leader, promised his citizens with all the authority of a Confucian father of the people is a chimera. It was his prophecy that all North Koreans would "wear silk clothes, eat white rice with meat soup every day, and live in well-heated tile-roofed homes" (quoted by Cha, p. 187). That more than half-a-century-old promise is vastly further from fulfillment today than when it was made.

Meanwhile, the Korean cousins of the South live with contemporary education of and about everything that is happening in the world. They have the freedom and resources to choose from the myriad of ways available to engage with the world's offerings. Their financial wellbeing, though subject to the ups and downs of capitalism, is hugely richer than those of the deprived North. The ROK has a sturdy democratic system of government and its citizens have constitutionally-articulated rights, liberties, and opportunities galore. South Korea ranks with Japan and many European countries with regard to prosperity and quality-of-life amenities. What, then, does the future hold for the increasingly differentiated Korean people who share life on the Korean Peninsula? Definitive prediction is not possible, but it is necessary to look ahead to the prospects for the future.

CHAPTER 7: FROM KIM TO KIM: SUCCESSION IN THE DPRK

Kim Jong II and the DPRK wanted the benefits of the Agreed Framework negotiated with the Clinton administration, but to receive them without giving up its nuclear weapons potential and its development of offensive missiles. A skeptical Bush administration came to the conclusion in 2002 that the DPRK was covertly engaged in a second nuclear program, using uranium rather than plutonium. Bush, calling out the DPRK as part of an "Axis of Evil," halted heavy fuel oil shipments to the DPRK, and the UN's International Atomic Energy Agency (IAEA) demanded honest scrutiny of the DPRK facilities. Instead, the DPRK publicized the restarting of its Yongbyon reactor.

In February 2005, just as the DPRK foreign ministry made its most definitive statement to date that they possessed nuclear weapons, the threat of North Korea proliferating nuclear materials to others came into stark relief when the White House officials Michael Green and William Tobey undertook a mission to Beijing, Seoul, and Tokyo to convey U.S. concerns that, sometime in 2004, Libya received nearly two tons of uranium hexafluoride suspected to be of North Korean origin ... The following month, Pyongyang asserted its sovereign right to test its long-range missiles, and in

April, it did not deny that it would sell its wares to terrorists if pushed into a corner by the United States. Between 2003 and 2005, it also undertook a massive reprocessing campaign, fueling and then defueling the Yongbyon reactor with batches of eight thousand fuel rods, which were then culled for their plutonium. According to experts, the North now had amassed an additional five to eight bombs worth of plutonium. The Bush administration's mantra henceforth was that it would not negotiate anything with North Korea except the 'complete, verifiable, and irreversible dismantlement' (CVID) of its nuclear programs (Cha, p. 256).

The Bush administration then initiated a new approach to negotiations with the DPRK. Finding its bilateral relationship unproductive and not always compatible with ROK-DPRK negotiations (the Roh administration preferred a softer line), the Bush team initiated an effort to engage in six-party talks with Japan, China, and Russia at the table with the US, ROK, and DPRK. While the arrangement would give the DPRK allies in the negotiation, the US, ROK, and Japan would be able to hold Russia and China accountable for whatever could be negotiated. Although the pace of accomplishment was tedious and slow, there was progress that produced a six-party joint statement in September 2005. Its significant assertions included the following:

- The DPRK would abandon nuclear weapons and programs and submit to IAEA safeguards.

- The US would not attack or invade the DPRK.

- The ROK would not have or use nuclear weapons.

- The denuclearization of weapons would extend throughout the Korean Peninsula.

- The US would express respect for the DPRK's right to peaceful uses of nuclear energy.

Although the agreement was vague, lacking in specificity,

it was widely applauded as a positive step toward world peace. In South Korea and Japan, there was positive relief from an apparent easing of regional tensions. Encouragement was taken from the fact that the US and China had accomplished an affirmative agreement through a lengthy consultative process. The apparent success of the six-party negotiations led to optimism regarding future cooperation in Asia.

The afterglow from the agreement was brief. The US indicated that the light water reactors for the DPRK's peaceful use of energy would come *at an appropriate time*. The US notion of *appropriate* was not until North Korea had "eliminated all nuclear weapons and all nuclear programs, and this has been verified to the satisfaction of all parties by credible international means, including the IAEA; and when the DPRK has come into full compliance with the NPT [Non-Proliferation Treaty] and IAEA safeguards, and has demonstrated a sustained commitment to cooperation and transparency and has ceased proliferating nuclear technology" (Oberdorfer and Carlin, quoting a US closing statement on September 19, 2005, pp. 406-407). The DPRK responded by calling the United States' statement a retreat from its commitments and that the DPRK would not move forward on denuclearization.

The US Treasury Department made its own intrusive move against the DPRK at about the same time. A deep investigation of financial transactions conducted abroad in US dollars discovered that DPRK enterprises were circulating counterfeit American hundred dollar bills and laundered money through a Macau bank (Banco Delta Asia, or BDA). A Treasury Department advisory to US banks to not to do business with Banco Delta Asia followed.

> Upon learning that one of their banks was designated by the U. S. Treasury Department as a money launderer, Macau regulatory authorities immediately took control of the bank and froze for investigation all North Korean accounts, amounting to about $25 million. Moreover, once other

bank presidents and bank regulators around the world learned of the Section 311 [a provision of the US Patriot Act of Congress], they, too, sought to freeze or expel all North Korean assets in their banks. While this action had little effect on the average North Korean (who does not have overseas bank accounts or hard currency), it had a dramatic impact on the elite, who suddenly found that they could not access their stashes of cash around the world. The North Korean leadership quickly learned that there was only one thing potentially worse than losing their nuclear weapons, and that was losing their financial reputation. Accounts were frozen (Cha, pp. 264-265).

The banking sanctions, small in world trade terms, did constitute sanctions on Kim Jong Il and his elite supporters. In Cha's judgment, "North Korea's response to BDA triggered the third nuclear crisis." In July 2006, the DPRK fired off seven ballistic missiles. One failed in flight but six came down in the Sea of Japan, east of the Russian coast. In October, the DPRK announced an upcoming nuclear bomb test, following up in a week at Punggye. Thus the DPRK confirmed its ability to produce and explode a plutonium nuclear device as well as deliver it by rocket.

In response to these unprecedented acts, the UN Security Council passed two resolutions (UNSCR 1695 and UNSCR 1718) condemning Pyongyang, and implementing a range of sanctions against it. These resolutions also marked the first time that China and Russia, two traditionally close allies of the North, signed on to Security Council resolutions against the regime (Cha, p. 267).

The support for the UN sanctions given by Russia and China in the Security Council was taken as a hopeful sign that North Korea's nuclear efforts could and would be subject to controls from these allies. If Russia, and especially China, would participate in hard-edged sanctions against the DPRK, the threat level, though real, would be reduced among all the Asian neighbors.

Commentators differ in their judgment about the practical effects of the sanctions. According to Lankov, "Even though they professed to participate in the sanctions regime, the Chinese did not let it influence their position: on the contrary, 2006, the year of the first nuclear test, also marked an upsurge in the scale of Chinese aid to and economic cooperation with Pyongyang – and this scale has been increasing ever since" (Lankov, p. 156). According to Cha, who was part of the Bush team, "Beijing did take tougher measures, most of which took place out of the public eye ... It also curtailed economic and political cooperation through unseen but all-important party-to-party channels and PLA-to-KPA (People's Liberation Army-to-Korean People's Army) channels. But it hardly abandoned the regime" (Cha, p. 268).

After loosening its control over the $25 million previously withheld from the DPRK by the US, the six-party talks, hosted by China, resumed and a process began in which the DPRK agreed to dismantle its Yongbyon reactor in 2008. There would be site visits for inspections and a verification process. The US would remove the DPRK from its terrorism list and restart shipments of heavy fuel oil to supply North Korea's power generation needs. A substantial beginning of the dismantlement in Yongbyon went forward, but inspections and searches of the documents for all the DPRK's nuclear programs convinced the US that the DPRK was cheating. It would not own up to evidence of highly enriched uranium. The US, in turn, refused to delist North Korea from its terrorism status. North Korea responded by abruptly ending the disablement of its outdated Yongbyon facilities. In the meantime, it became known that Kim Jong Il had suffered a stroke.

Negotiations on the issues collapsed and the issue disappeared with the US presidential election about to take place. The Bush administration was running out of time. "In an early warning of what was to come, one ranking North

Korean official told an American in a private conversation soon after the US elections that the situation was already out of the hands of the diplomats ... Decisions sure to cause problems with United States had been reached at the top levels in Pyongyang, and there was nothing that could be done about it" (Oberdorfer and Carlin, p. 431).

As a South Korean observer declared:

Pyongyang can be said to have gone much further in the disablement process than in the first US-DPRK nuclear standoff [with the Clinton administration], only to receive much less in return. Pyongyang had gained neither promises of normalization nor even any glimmer of hope for the light water reactors, though these had been part of the AF [Agreed Framework under Clinton]. It is no surprise that the voices in Pyongyang saying that engagement policies were ineffective became louder (Kim, Samuel S., p. 78).

In 2007, a political newcomer and freshman US Senator was positioning himself for future possibilities. This mostly unknown Democrat, Barack Obama, offered his take on making peace in East Asia. Obama expressed high-minded aspirations about handling the challenges with the East Asian countries, both the US allies and rival China. The opportunities for successful peacemaking seemed palpable to him at the time.

As China rises and Japan and South Korea assert themselves, I will work to forge a more effective framework in Asia that goes beyond bilateral agreements, occasional summits, and ad hoc arrangements, such as the six-party talks on North Korea. We need an inclusive infrastructure with the countries in East Asia that can promote stability and prosperity and help confront transnational threats, from terrorist cells in the Philippines to avian flu in Indonesia. I will also encourage China to play a responsible role as a growing power—to help lead in addressing the common problems of the twenty-first century. We will compete with China in some areas and cooperate in others. Our essential challenge is to build a relationship that broadens cooperation while strengthening our ability to compete (Obama, *Foreign Affairs*, July/August 2007).

There was another side to the Bush administration than the hard bargaining it conducted to produce denuclearization. With the support of Congress, Bush initiated a North Korean Human Rights Act in 2004 and had it renewed in 2008. It offered food aid and refugee assistance to the people of North Korea. It even brought nearly a hundred North Korean refugees to the United States by 2010.

> In May 2008 the U. S. Agency for International Development started a major food aid program of 500,000 metric tons for the North but only after adequate access and monitoring was allowed for the NGO [non-government organization] consortium and the WFP [World Food Programme] participants. Seventy-five inspectors in nine field offices were offered unprecedented access, especially with the permitted use of Korean-speakers ... [But] the North abruptly ended this in March 2009, with only a little more than 130,000 tons received, as tensions grew worse on the nuclear front (Cha, p. 205).

North Korea's continuing insistence to have and develop its nuclear weapons prevented a sincere effort at humanitarian assistance to North Korea's hungry people.

After regaining strength following his stroke, Kim Jong Il apparently came to his conclusion about a successor, choosing the youngest of his three sons. Kim Jong Un received appointments matching those his father had received a generation before: "[T]he young man was given the rank of four-star general in September 2010 though he had never served in the military. He was also made the number two in the Central Military Committee of the [Korean Workers'] Party" (Cha, p. 98). In the following year, father and son were seen together regularly, doing inspection visits to factories, towns, and military centers. "In May 2011, as a test, it appears Kim Jong Un was left in charge of the country when his father traveled to China. When the senior Kim's train returned, the son greeted it at the station, and North Korean television showed high-level cadre bowing low to the younger man as they emerged from the train" (Oberdorfer and Carlin, p. 453). As Cha points out, "for the world, and for the North Korean people, Kim Jong-un's appearance was clearly calculated to look like the spitting image of his grandfather some sixty years prior, when the Soviets first unveiled Kim Il-sung to the North Korean people" (Cha, pp. 99-100).

In January 2009, the United States celebrated the inauguration of President Barack Obama and a new Democratic administration. One of the quotable lines in his inaugural speech was to say to unfriendly nations, "we will extend a hand if you are willing to unclench your fist." North Korea's response was a hostile announcement of upcoming long-range missile tests. The Obama administration pointed out that such a launch would violate United Nations' sanctions. But, bold as brass, in April, the DPRK sent its missile successfully into the Sea of Japan. The UN Security Council condemned the act, a condemnation joined by both China and Russia. The DPRK announced its withdrawal from future six-party talks and declared it would not be bound by previously agreed terms. Instead, it would restart its nuclear plant in Yongbyon. In short order, the DPRK conducted a successful nuclear blast in May that, from technical tracings, was estimated to be in the range of six kilotons. Shown the fist, not the hand, the new US president and North Korea were quickly at an impasse.

The new administration said it would have a "strategic patience" policy. On October 29, 2009, Secretary of State Hillary Clinton asserted the US position. "North Korea's return to the negotiating table is not enough. Current sanctions will not be relaxed until Pyongyang takes verifiable, irreversible steps toward complete denuclearization. Its leaders should be under no illusion that the United States will ever have normal, sanctions-free relations with a nuclear-armed North Korea" (quoted in Kim, Samuel S., p. 80). On November 9, 2009, President Obama made a statement in Seoul with ROK President Lee at his side. "Our message is clear: If North Korea is prepared to take concrete and irreversible steps to fulfill its obligations and eliminate its nuclear weapons program, the United States will support economic assistance and help promote its full integration into the community of nations. That opportunity and respect will not come with threats – North Korea must live up to its obligations" (Cha, p. 314). Strategic patience meant that the US had other problems at home and abroad, and North Korea would be ignored until the DPRK expressed an affirmative interest in accepting the American terms for diplomacy.

Alienated from the Obama administration and the hardline regime in the ROK, Kim Jong Il welcomed enlarged relations with China.

> In October 2010, a delegation consisting of the party heads of every North Korean province went to Beijing, almost certainly an effort by Kim Jong Il to impress on provincial-level officials that they had to be ready for major interaction with Chinese businesses moving into their areas. In July 2011, groundbreaking ceremonies were held for new joint economic zones with the Chinese on several North Korean islands in the Yalu River, and the North signed the agreements with the Chinese for developing Rajin [a port city on the Sea of Japan] (Oberdorfer and Carlin, p. 448).

Oberdorfer and Carlin assert that Kim Jong Il had no other potential partner to turn to and, sensing the need to set things in order for his death and succession by Kim Jong Un, "he needed to secure ties with China on both strategic and economic fronts" (Oberdorfer and Carlin, p. 449).

Lankov observed: "After the nuclear test, the volume of trade between China and North Korea began to grow with remarkable speed, tripling throughout between 2006 and 2011" (Lankov, p. 176).

On December 19, 2011, an official announcement from the DPRK revealed the death of Kim Jong Il from a heart attack. After relative silence for more than a week, an elaborate funeral took place on December 28. *The New York Times* reported the details, excerpted here:

> On the surface, the funeral appeared to proceed with the precision of totalitarian choreography. Kim Jong-un walked with one hand on the hearse and the other raised in salute. Neat rows of soldiers in olive-green uniforms stood, hats off and bowing, in front of the Kumsusan mausoleum, where Kim Jong-Il's body had been lying in state since his death was announced on Dec. 19.

> When the funeral motorcade stopped before the soldiers at the start of a 25-mile procession through Pyongyang, they gave a last salute and a military band played the national anthem. Mr. Kim and other top officials did not walk the entire route; from inside their limousines, they watched crowds of citizens and soldiers wailing along the boulevards under a cold gray sky ...

> The funeral lasted three hours. The funeral, and the mourning, appeared to have been meticulously staged by the government to strengthen the cult of personality underpinning the Kim family's rule. State television and radio announcers exhorted North Koreans to support the family with their lives. They even attributed the heavy snowfall ahead of the funeral to 'heaven's grief' ...

> On Wednesday, *Rodong Sinmun*, the main newspaper of the Workers' Party, said the North's nuclear weapons program and long-range missile technology were among the biggest achievements

of Kim Jong II. 'Thanks to these legacies, we do not worry about the destiny of ourselves and posterity at this time of national mourning,' it said.

And on Thursday, as part of a memorial service that drew a large crowd to the main plaza in central Pyongyang, Kim Yong-nam, president of the North Korean Parliament, delivered a speech urging the military and people to rally around Kim Jong-un to 'solidify his monolithic leadership.'

'He is the supreme leader who inherits the ideology, leadership, courage and audacity of Comrade Kim Jong-il,' he said (Choe, *New York Times*, December 28, 2011).

The US and South Korean diplomats engaged in conversations of cautious concern about whether the leadership turnover in the North would cause the DPRK to strike out at South Korea. An American envoy touched base with China, requesting its attention to North Korea, lest matters go awry there, either internally or externally. The North Korean Central News Agency took umbrage at ROK President Lee Myung-bak for failing to express condolences regarding Kim's death, even threatening that North Korea could turn the South Korean Blue House into a sea of fire. The unknown nature of the new leader and his unpredictability gave the US and ROK administrations worried consideration. Kim Jong Un quickly took up the office of Supreme Leader of the Korean People's Army.

After the funeral was over, the younger Kim immediately began appearing in public, showing off his new, youthful, hands-on style of leadership. On the first day of the new year, he appeared at one of the Army's premier tank units. North Korean television showed Kim meticulously inspecting the base exactly as his father had done in the past, and then appearing with the soldiers who deliriously chanted his name (Oberdorfer and Carlin, pp. 453-454).

There were diplomatic contacts between the US and North Korean envoys in China during February 2012. Perhaps the two countries could develop some confidence building in the aftermath of leadership change in North Korea. Often after dramatic events, the DPRK would begin a charm offensive to get benefits from its rivals. The US had canceled food aid after the DPRK stopped its denuclearization program. Interestingly, as the conversation went back and forth, negotiators for the North even called upon the US to provide its aid in the form of grain. At the time, the US was defining food assistance as supplements, such as powdered milk that would most directly benefit needy children, not supply resources for foodstuffs going to the military or the economic elite of the country. The charm from the DPRK dissolved when it issued a warning about retaliatory strikes in case US-South Korean military exercises got close to the DPRK's coastal artillery. In March, the DPRK announced to American consternation an impending satellite launch to occur in April. A frustrated President Obama called upon China to restrain the DPRK's aggressive intentions. The DPRK went ahead with its launch, but was humiliated before fifty invited foreign journalists when the rocket to put the satellite in orbit ascended less than one hundred miles; to reach orbit, the satellite had to attain more than three hundred miles. Throughout the rest of the year, the relationship between the DPRK with the US and South Korea was mostly watchful waiting.

In 2013, a little more than two years after Kim succeeded his father, Jang Song-thaek, Kim's uncle, and two prominent deputies were executed. Jang was for years considered the second most powerful figure in the government, and he was conspicuously close to Kim during the funeral for Kim Jong Il. But in 2013, he was convicted of treason for having enlarged his power while profiteering from mineral exports and for plotting Kim's overthrow. He and his deputies were machinegunned to death. It is reported that Jang's name has been expurgated from official documents and that hundreds of his underlings were purged from their elite positions (Choe, *New York Times*, March 12, 2016). South Korean reports indicate that Kim promptly replaced nearly a third of the high party members, nearly half of the high military officers, and a quarter of the top government administrators (Joo, p. 32). Evidently, Kim emerged from the challenge better established as the regime's Great Successor.

In March 2013, the UN Human Rights Council decided upon an inquiry into the DPRK "to investigate the systematic, widespread and grave violations of human rights in the Democratic People's Republic of Korea, with a view to ensuring full accountability, in particular for violations which may amount to crimes against humanity." Unsurprisingly, the DPRK did not allow the commission members to enter and examine the situation on the ground in the country. It "totally and categorically" rejected cooperation with the commission of inquiry. The commission's report drew upon "more than 240 confidential interviews with victims and other witnesses." In 2014, when the commission released its report, it included a concise letter sent to the DPRK's "supreme leader" Kim Jong Un, requesting that he address detailed human rights abuses in North Korea. The UN Security Council passed a resolution to hold human rights violators, including Kim Jong Un, accountable for "crimes against humanity." (See Commission of Inquiry on Human Rights in the Democratic People's Republic of Korea (A/HRC/25/63) See more at **http:// www.ohchr.org/EN/HRBodies/HRC/CoIDPRK/Pages/ CommissionInquiryonHRinDPRK.aspx**)

The New York Times report included this summary report on the UN action.

> The resolution closely followed the recommendations of a commission of inquiry submitted last month that was considered the most authoritative assessment of human rights in North Korea. Led by a retired Australian judge, Michael Kirby, the commission documented in often gruesome detail violations ranging from the 'crime of extermination'

to the brutal conditions in concentration camps, including enslavement, torture, rape and persecution on grounds of race, religion and gender.

That report and, now, the resolution represent a concerted effort by rights activists and United Nations human rights officials to broaden the focus of international attention from North Korea's nuclear policies and to include decades of abuse on a scale that Navi Pillay, the organization's human rights chief, has remarked 'has no parallel anywhere in the world.'

In compiling the report, the commission wrote to Kim Jong-un, North Korea's leader, advising him that he might be held personally liable in court for crimes against humanity committed by state institutions and officials under his direct control (Cumming-Bruce, *New York Times*, March 28, 2014).

This commission report has sustained the continuing imposition of international sanctions on North Korea. The lack of any positive response or remorse by the DPRK's young Supreme Leader was a disappointment to UN participants, but not really unexpected. However, China, the DPRK's chief enabler, seemed embarrassed by the DPRK's low standing as publicized in the international condemnation of its human rights record. In July 2014, Xi Jinping, China's president, in a noticeable snub, bypassed the North to consult in Seoul with South Korea about increasing their bilateral trade relations.

What commentators see as the DPRK's pattern of international relations is captured this way:

The 'Pyongyang Playbook' goes as follows: Offer a fake overture of peace; raise the stakes for your foes with a provocation; act unstable and threaten to escalate even further; and finally, call for talks and act reasonable. Pyongyang seizes and maintains the initiative from beginning to end and leaves its adversaries anxious for negotiations in the face of provocations (Lee and Stanton, *Foreign Affairs,* September 14, 2015).

In contrast to Obama's optimism in 2007 and his open hand offer in his inaugural speech, by the middle of his second term, after ups and downs of responding to North Korea's occasional charm offensives and then to its upraised fist, Obama had largely withdrawn into his policy of "strategic patience." In contrast, Obama's mostly Republican critics wanted him to "do something, don't just stand there." For the most part, the US was in fact dealing with North Korea by maintaining approximate unity with both Japan and South Korea. Exercising togetherness, they maintained a multilateral, mostly economic, sanction effort against the North.

Japan and its prime minister, Shinzo Abe, have had a unique issue to negotiate with the DPRK. Decades ago, North Korea abducted about a dozen Japanese citizens. In 2002, the North Koreans admitted to the abductions, even revealing that the abductees had been used to prepare DPRK spies for undercover work against Japan. So despite North Korea's nuclear threat and its missiles splashing into the Sea of Japan, in 2014, Abe was willing to loosen Japan's regulations against North Korean shipping in Japanese waters and allow some economic exchanges in return for North Korea's resolving the abducted citizens' plight. In May 2014, after bilateral talks between Japan and the DPRK were held in Stockholm, the Abe government claimed an agreement. It would lift a ban on travel between the two countries, allow financial transfers, and admit North Korean ships into Japanese ports. In response, North Korea would investigate and reveal the fate of the mysteriously abducted Japanese citizens who had been hijacked from Japan by Korean agents during the 1970s and 1980s. Survivors, if any, would be returned and full information about the rest would be shared. Prime Minister Abe claimed a significant "mission accomplished" by making the deal. Some observers considered this a hopeful sign that the new Kim Jong

Un regime would open up civil relations with its neighbors. However, by February 2016, Japan, having received little or nothing from North Korea, changed tactics. In the wake of the 2016 nuclear test in North Korea, followed by its rocket launching of a satellite, Japan said it would reimpose its previous sanctions and it has done so.

The DPRK provocations that so offended Japan in 2016 also incited retribution from the Park administration in South Korea. In February 2016, South Korea closed the Kaesong industrial complex, a step of finality after a dozen years of that special industrial sanctuary remaining operational despite many inter-Korean insults and acts of hostility. The small- to medium-sized South Korean-owned enterprises employed about fifty thousand North Koreans, mostly women, in a wide variety of manufacturing jobs. About a thousand South Koreans managed 120 business operations. South Korea announced the shutdown on February 10. The very next day, the DPRK sent all the South Koreans packing and confiscated all the assets left behind (*The Chosun Ilbo*, February 25, 2016). The investment loss to South Korea was estimated at about $650 million.

Interestingly, South Korean commentary on the closing suggested that the DPRK's new young leader was chalking up one more conspicuous achievement in preparation for a North Korean Workers' Party Congress, upcoming in May 2016 – the first such North Korean Party Congress in thirty-six years. Ironically, the North Koreans responded to the South's latest sanctions with this statement by its Committee for the Peaceful Reunification of the Fatherland: "From this moment, we declare all the inter-Korean agreements on economic cooperation and exchange null and void" (*The Chosun Ilbo,* March 11, 2016).

The US, generally (and President Obama in particular), was largely silent regarding North Korean initiatives during the first third of 2016. The president seemed content with "leading from behind." Secretary of State John Kerry responded to the DPRK's January nuclear test by saying that the US "will do what is necessary to protect the people of our country." Peculiarly, that observation was expressed in Beijing, where Kerry sought to put the burden of changing North Korea's bad behavior on the People's Republic of China. Kerry exhorted China, North Korea's primary trading partner, to pressure the North Koreans into giving up their nuclear weapons and capacity to create and deliver more. China, more than North Korea, can be subjected to either or both economic measures and military weaponry by the United States. Banking controls, effectively imposed upon Iran for a long time, could crack down on China's financial transactions on behalf of North Korea. On the military side, the US developed a missile-defense system called THAAD (Terminal High Altitude Area Defense), which could be deployed in South Korea and Japan; something China would consider an imposition upon its own military capabilities (Perlez and Sanger, *New York Times*, January 27, 2016).

The South Korean press reported extensively about the prospects for the placement of a THAAD antimissile battery in the ROK, discussing alternate locations and timing for the installation. President Park's public perspective became favorable about having THAAD placements in the ROK after the North Korean nuclear test took place in January. Pollsters quickly measured public opinion in South Korea, reporting:

> 67.1 percent [of respondents] support the US Forces Korea's deployment of THAAD batteries here. Some 26.2 percent are against due to the potential damage to Seoul-Beijing relations ... Only 29.3 percent [express support] for South Korea developing its [own] nuclear weapons and 23.2 percent [are] for the redeployment of tactical U.S. nuclear weapons here, while 41.1 percent want South Korea to remain free of nuclear weapons (*The Chosun Ilbo,* February, 16, 2016).

Clearly, North Korea's neighbors are frustrated with its recalcitrance about nuclear weapons and missile delivery systems. There is also authentic compassion for the North Korean people, largely unknowing victims of a self-centered elite that deprives them of the benefits that could come in response to transparency about nuclear disarmament. Certainly it is the case that optimism is needed to stimulate conciliation between the two Koreas. Their neighbors and the US would go to great lengths to make a peaceful transition go smoothly. But optimism alone is insufficient. Nearly two decades ago, when Kim Dae Jong was pushing the Sunshine Policy, his minister of foreign affairs and trade offered the following analysis, which is perhaps both valid and yet unfulfilled. As of mid-2017, it is still difficult to discern a path to peace on the Korean Peninsula. Much ink has been spilled trying to articulate a reasonable and promising trajectory, but for more than half a century, the interactions of the international participants have been circuitous and disappointing. Perhaps the cautious optimism of the ROK's minister for foreign aid and trade from the Kim Dae Jong administration should still be noted and patiently followed.

> While there has been much speculation about North Korean collapse in recent years, it is unlikely to come anytime soon. The communists' airtight grip on all manner of social, economic, political, and military affairs has so far ensured their stability and may well continue to do so. Meanwhile, South Korea does not seek the North's collapse and has officially proclaimed this position; a breakdown in the North could open up military, political, and humanitarian pitfalls. It is therefore simply too dangerous to count on the North's collapse as the key to the nation's future. South Korea aims to achieve peace and reunification methodically and gradually instead. This will take time — perhaps a long time — but it will be worth the wait. And it is the only viable course to pursue ...

> It may be a long time before North Korea recognizes these truths and comes to share the same

values as the South. Full reconciliation will therefore have to wait. Two divided entities can embark on the process of unification only after they reach a consensus on how to unify and how to live together afterward. A reunited Korea is thus a long-term prospect. But when it comes, the gradual and peaceful unification should be welcomed by the United States, China, Russia, and Japan, for it will defuse a dangerous flash point and create an expanded market for their goods and services ...

To further this process of integration, unified Korea should aspire to be non-nuclear and peaceful, limiting its armory to conventional weapons. It must respect its existing borders. Unified Korea will remain an integral part of the world economy, however, playing by global rules and standards. If managed properly, the peaceful unification of Korea will be a historic turning point, stamping out the final smoldering legacy of the Cold War (Hong, *Foreign Affairs*, 1999).

Unfortunately, the DPRK's third Kim seems to have solidified his standing as the "Great Successor" and his early moves do not seem to auger well for the likelihood that peace is around the corner. Having weathered what some thought would be a precarious transition, Kim's potential longevity makes the probability of substantial reconciliation on the peninsula rather doubtful in the near term. But instead of closing on this pessimistic note, the next chapter draws together recent views from prominent commentators about the future in the Korean Peninsula.

CHAPTER 8: ONE KOREA OR TWO?

One Korea, the dependency subject to Japan during the first half of the twentieth century, became two Koreas, North and South, by the arbitrary division imposed by the Soviet Union and the United States in 1945. The matter was at the time merely a minor consideration in the peace arrangements that the major powers negotiated as World War II came to an end. The Korean War of the early 1950s froze a developing hostile relationship into place. The North promptly collectivized into Stalinist communism. The South more slowly implemented capitalism and representational democracy. More than seventy years on, that separation continues with the demarcation at the 38th parallel, a matter settled only by an armistice agreement, not a treaty of peace. Moreover, there is a history of provocations initiated by one side or the other. Usually, the DPRK has been the aggressor and its forays have even included attempts to assassinate two of the South's presidents. There have been peace initiatives from time to time but they have never brought a fruitful conclusion.

The ROK has established and funded an enduring agency optimistically entitled The Ministry of Unification. For many years, it has articulated reunification policy and addressed in careful language responses to "inter-Korean policy issues." It constantly monitors activities in the DPRK which may help/hinder the likelihood of a peaceful unification in the future. To illustrate its efforts, consider excerpts from its

2013 White Paper on Korean Unification that summarizes its mission and its approaches.

> [T]he ROK government proposed the Vision 3000 initiative, a bold plan to foster a favorable environment in the North so that it will dismantle its nuclear program. In return for any progress in denuclearization, the ROK and the international community would work out a comprehensive package (covering the five key areas of economy, education, finance, infrastructure and standard of living) to help North Korea upgrade its economy by achieving an annual per-capita income of USD 3,000 in just ten years, and improve the standard of living of its people. In summary, Vision 3000 clearly and strategically lays out the benefits for North Korea if it cooperates.

> Second, the ROK is working to build a healthy and normal relationship with North Korea through mutually beneficial cooperation and respect ... On the subject of inter-Korean dialogue, the ROK government has underscored the need for sincere discussions, rather than engaging in dialogue for the sake of dialogue ... It has already been proven that building a relationship through one-sided assistance is not sustainable. Thus, the ROK government worked to bring progress through exchange, cooperation and assistance, and to build a relationship that is mutually beneficial.

> Third, the ROK government has been guided by universal values in executing its unification policy. In the course of world history, democratic freedom, human rights, and market economy have emerged as universally accepted values ... Thus, the South has remained committed to addressing the issues of separated families, South Korean prisoners of war, and abductees from a humanitarian perspective.

Finally, the government began making substantial preparations for unification in earnest.... The government established five tasks that are vital for achieving this goal (promoting public support for unification, raising unification funds, actively engaging in unification diplomacy, embracing victims of separation, and laying the necessary institutional groundwork), and has worked consistently to bring them into the public forum (*2013 White Paper on Korean Unification*, pp. 15-16).

Interestingly, the DPRK has not been silent on the matter of peace, unification, and nuclear weapons. The DPRK sponsors a Korean Friendship Association and has an easily accessed website for Americans (www.kfaus.org), where it has posted an "Open Letter to the South Korean Side," posted on January 25, 2014, that reproduces a letter sent on January 23, 2014, from the National Defense Commission (NDC) of the DPRK, authorized by its Supreme Commander Kim Jong Un. Excerpts say the following:

> The history of the territorial partition which has lasted for several decades has brought untold misfortune and pain to the Korean nation ... Firmly determined to put an end to the history of the territorial partition and national split in view of the hard reality to which the Korean nation can no longer remain a passive on-looker, the supreme leadership of the DPRK in the New Year Address clarified internally and externally realistic ways of opening a fresh phase of national reunification ...

> The important proposal of the DPRK reflects the steadfast will of its army and people to improve the north-south relations by concerted efforts of the two sides, not asking about all inglorious happenings in the past ... The north-south relations will be improved on a solid basis only when both sides take realistic measures to prevent impending nuclear disasters with concerted efforts of the Korean nation. The denuclearization of the

Korean Peninsula is a goal common to the nation as it should be realized by concerted efforts of all Koreans ...

Unshakable is the stand of the service personnel and people of the DPRK to pave a wide avenue for mending the north-south relations by concerted efforts of the Korean nation. Improved inter-Korean relations precisely mean the independent reunification, peace and prosperity desired by all Koreans (News (http://www. kfausa.org/category/news/), Reunification).

Taking the expressions of the two sides seriously could someday lead to denuclearization, unification, and societal peace. Perhaps there is encouragement to be taken from knowing that both sides continue to express interest in unification, something only possible through negotiation, compromise, and mutually agreed-upon sacrifices. The absence of much progress toward peacemaking and unification may indicate that the declarations above are mere propaganda. Or it may be that there are hopeful peacemakers in both countries but they cannot control the political leadership of their respective countries. Nevertheless, in the contemporary setting, there is not a great deal of optimism among those closest to the continuing strife between the North and the South to expect denuclearization, unification, and societal peace very soon.

Although there are huge differences between the two Korean republics — the ROK having a prosperous economy within an orderly and well governed society, and the DPRK suffering economic depression and constant decline — the DPRK is not a "failed state." An accepted definition of that concept is:

A state in which one or more of the fundamental conditions of sovereign government are absent (see sovereignty). These conditions include the presence of a recognized government, that government's monopoly on the legitimate use of physical force, the provision of basic public services, and the ability to represent that country on the international stage. The absence of these conditions is common in countries experiencing civil war, a military invasion, or a major dispute over the location of political borders (*Oxford Dictionary of Human Geography*, 2013).

That is not the DPRK's condition. As unsuccessful as it appears to Western eyes in meeting the needs of its people for liberty, health, and prosperous living, the ruling elite does carry out typical governing activities, maintains an effective military, defends its borders, provides its society a unique ideology, and enforces a rule of law for civil order. Indeed, the regime underwent a turnover of its "Dear Leader" and then successfully put in place its third-generation "Great Successor," Kim Jong Un, who appears to be firmly ensconced as the accepted leader. He is seems to be functioning with apparent acceptance and wide approval from the North Korean people.

Can that level of success continue indefinitely? Expert opinion is in general agreement. Andrei Lankov answers that question without ambivalence or equivocating: "There is little doubt that in the long run the current North Korean regime is doomed. Its innate – and incurable – economic inefficiency and the resulting inability to decrease the steadily growing income gap with its neighbors (especially South Korea) is its Achilles heel" (Lankov, p. 233). He anticipates the "likely collapse" of the Kim family regime because the North Korean people will come to realize how badly off they are. However, he suggests no timeline for that event. He does predict, however, that cleaning up the "mess" will take decades.

Cha, whose in-depth study of North Korea has often been quoted in previous chapters, provides a more nuanced evaluation. Having considered the initial success of Kim Jong Un, he expresses this judgment: "Despite what appears to be a stable power transition to a new generation of Kim-family rule, I still believe that a dead-end awaits the regime"

(Cha, p. 468). But when? Near the conclusion of his book, he says:

> What I have offered in these pages is based on my study of the country as a scholar and my interaction with the regime during my period of service in the U.S. Government. Even then I cannot tell you with any degree of certainty what will happen tomorrow in this country. If you were to open your paper at your doorstep tomorrow morning, or turn on your computer with your morning coffee, and find a headline that informed you the DPRK has had collapsed, I would have to admit that I would not be surprised. But if ten years from now the regime has outlived my predictions of serious crisis, I would also tell you that I am not surprised. The range of probability regarding the DPRK's ultimate fate is that wide. In this sense, it is truly the impossible state (Cha, p. 462).

In a wryly titled piece, "The Long Goodbye: The Future of North Korea," Kaplan and Denmark likewise see the end of the DPRK as unavoidable. After careful rumination about the regime, its history, and international context, they consider its demise to be certain.

> Yet one way or another, we have to assume that the status quo will not last forever, and regime change will alter the power arrangements in Northeast Asia, where there has been peace and prosperity despite the tensions caused by the presence of a weapons-hungry Stalinist regime brutalizing its people. But this Cold War-style standoff, peaceful as it has largely been, cannot last indefinitely (Kaplan and Denmark, p. 21).

Experts agree that North Korea's days are numbered, but no one can confidently forecast when the present regime will dissolve.

Is there any consensus about the DPRK's nuclear arms and its missiles? What is beyond dispute is the DPRK has successfully developed its nuclear resources and actually weaponized them. Successful underground explosions have been documented in 2006, 2009, 2012, and January 2016. Likewise, there have been missile tests, not all of them successful, but the evidence is clear that South Korea, Japan, and the Philippines are within the reach of the DPRK's rocketry. Despite many false disclaimers in the past about its intentions to build weapons, the DPRK proudly and publicly exults in its weapons today, forecasts its tests, and publicizes its successes. Its neighbors can only cry foul and vainly protest to the United Nations without much further success in penalizing the Kim government.

Given the DPRK's successes at nuclearization, it seems apparent that the genie can hardly be put back in the bottle. Lankov argues that "the complete, verifiable and irreversible" denuclearization that the US has seeks is doomed to remain unattainable as long as the Kim family regime is in control of the DPRK (Lankov, p. 253). He advises the US and North Korea's neighbors to adopt a de facto acceptance of its nuclear arms and offer material incentives to obtain an agreement freezing in place its current weapons. The US would mitigate the DPRK's threat by paying it not to make its stockpile of arms larger and more powerful. Even assuming that degree of success, he acknowledges, North Korea would be rewarded for successful blackmail. That, of course, may well not be politically feasible in the democratic nations where leaders hold office only at the sufferance of popular elections.

Cha argues that of course the DPRK's neighbors must continue stern sanctions to restrict the choices made by North Korean leaders. However, diplomacy is the primary instrument for obtaining denuclearization.

> The DPRK will continue to keep their actual nuclear weapons as the last bargaining chip in any negotiation. Thus, any attempts at a 'mega-deal' that offers more incentives to get more in return may sound great, but these are all eventually whittled down by the North to smaller steps

To borrow football analogy, negotiating with North Korea is not done with the eighty-yard-long pass. It is a ground game, where you are fighting to get one yard at a time (Cha, p. 458).

A South Korean perspective offers this wisdom. The options for dealing with North Korea distill into three: "a hawkish approach, strategic patience, and sequential engagement" (Joo, p. 33). Regarding the hawkish approach, he notes that the hard-edged measures by the Bush administration were unsuccessful in halting the DPRK's moves forward in nuclearization. The contrasting approach by the Obama administration applying "strategic patience" lost ground to the DPRK as well. "While Washington may have been strategically patient, Pyongyang has been strategically impatient, initiating a series of military provocations, missile launches, and a nuclear test" (Joo, p. 33). Like Lankov and Cha, Joo would rely upon negotiation, specifically "sequential engagement." Having closely considered the pace and contents of North Korean communications directed at the US in the last two decades, Joo thinks that the DPRK "might agree to denuclearization in return for normalization" (Joo, p. 34). Normalization with the US means that "Washington should be prepared to replace the current armistice agreement with a peace treaty and establish diplomatic relations by exchanging ambassadors" (Joo, p. 34). Joo sees this outcome as the result of three affirmative steps by the US. First, a pledge of no hostile intent by the US regarding the DPRK. Second, promising "not to launch a nuclear attack on North Korea unless North Korea makes the first move." Third, exchange normalization for denuclearization. The US should drop its negative labels for North Korea – a pariah regime, a rogue nation, an axis of evil. The US and its allies should assume as its default policy that engagement will lead to denuclearization. Joo concludes as follows:

> To assume that Pyongyang will never denuclear-
> ize will become a self-fulfilling prophecy. Indeed,
> such a belief would leave us with only two policy
> options: (1) live with a nuclear North Korea; or

(2) carry out a full-scale military invasion (regime change) or a surgical strike to force denucleariza-tion. Since both options are obviously out of the question, we should pursue sequential engage-ment – no matter how difficult, unpopular, or unattractive that policy may be. The art of poli-cymaking is to avoid the worst-case when better options are not feasible (Joo. p. 34).

The Pentagon, of course, surely does have on its shelf mil-itary options including surgical strike plans for North Korea that are not "out of the question," but the provocations that would trigger their use have not crossed a hypothetical red line. What has been missing to make a successful negotia-tion has been strong support for denuclearization from the DPRK's crucial allies, Russia and the People's Republic of China.

Russia has been inconspicuous regarding the nuclear issues between the US and North Korea. Cha observed that during the Bush administration, "Russia's part in the North Korean problem is best described as a bit player" (Cha, p. 367), although he related an incident of Russian helpful-ness during 2006 negotiations. More recently, however, a 2015 visit by Kim Jong Un to Russia for face-to-face con-sultations with Vladimir Putin suggests some reopening of bilateral relations between Russia and North Korea. The likely motivation for such a Russian initiative: "Russian relations with North Korea are good because [Russian] relations with United States are bad" (Jackson, 2015). It is the intensifying heat in the US-Russia relations – US dis-approval of Russian adventures in Syria and Ukraine – that prompted Putin to help prop up the Kim regime. "Russia may even see potential for North Korea to open up a new front of crisis or limited conflict that draws US attention away from what it does on the European periphery." The reopening initiative came from Putin to the DPRK – cancel-ing the old North Korean debts, reportedly a price of $10 billion. Of course, those debts are decades old and were uncollectible anyway. Jackson argues that "North Korea's significance to Russia is mostly limited to being a thorn in the United States' side." As a trading partner, Putin can give the DPRK an economic shot in the arm, thereby extending the time of the Kim regime's survival. Nevertheless, in the larger scheme of international rivalry, North Korea provides little for Putin to solve his more serious problems.

> Today's muscular Russia is actually in structural decline, and Putin's actions have unwittingly yielded a Ukraine more ethnically homogeneous and more Western-oriented than ever before. Moscow has tense relations with nearly every one of its neighbors and even with its biggest trading partners, including most recently Turkey. Even Germany, Russia's most important foreign policy counterpart and one of its most important economic partners, has had enough, backing sanctions at a cost to its own domestic situation (Kotkin, 2016).

There is little reason to suggest that Putin will have any interest in playing a positive role, at least in the near term, to encourage North Korea to give up its nuclear arms and establish a peaceful relationship with South Korea.

The relationship of the People's Republic of China with the DPRK is a complex and dynamic matter that reflects history, culture, socialistic ideology, trade, economic development, and international aspirations and rivalries. China paid a huge price in lives and treasure to save the DPRK from defeat in the Korean War. A decade later, in 1962, China settled a treaty with the DPRK "for the explicit purpose of cementing a permanent zone of peace on [its] northeast border. China, a country with centuries of border disputes with others surrounding it, values this border as permanent and unchanging" (Cha, p. 342). South of that border, China's dependency has served for seventy years as a buffer against any possible incursion by the United States and the ROK. China and the DPRK became established with and through communist ideology and collectivized economies. Although their economic systems have evolved differently, the rich mineral resources of Korea have a ready buyer in China, and China conveniently has all the goods that North Korea can pay for. Cha notes, in fact, that over forty percent of "Chinese joint ventures in North Korea are extractive industries" (Cha, p. 337). China has become an international leading power, but it continues to be the DPRK's only patron. China stands up for its small, unruly neighbor in a fashion unmatched by any other nation. Yet over time there have been uneven interactions between the two countries. China has normalized its relationships with the DPRK's chief rival, the ROK. The DPRK's adventurism with nuclear weapons and missiles has increased the possibility for military conflict that could spread throughout northeast Asia. That is, to China, a most unwelcome prospect. Scholarly observations suggests

> the North Korean nuclear threat has prompted Tokyo and Seoul to introduce ballistic-missile defenses, much to China's displeasure. Beijing has apparently calculated, however, that these disadvantages are outweighed by the risk of regime collapse in North Korea, which would entail a large number of refugees entering northern China, and the likelihood of a reunified Korean Peninsula under Seoul's control and allied with the United States. The prospect of a US military ally as China's direct neighbor, and possibly US troops on its borders, is deeply alarming to Beijing (Plant and Rhode, pp. 61-62).

What is the benefit to South Korea and the US if the Chinese succeed in their desire to keep the DPRK viable? The single benefit worth having is a North Korea without nuclear arms. China's desire for peaceful stability in northeast Asia can allow it to bring about a better level of economic prosperity in its relatively undeveloped provinces of Liaoning and Jillin. That would increase wealth and economic well-being on both sides of the China-North Korea border to the benefit of both the Chinese and the North Korean people. It would, of course, improve the viability of the Kim regime.

Given time and continuing stability in its relations with North Korea, China could mentor North Korea into an economy of state capitalism as the Chinese practice it at home. That could gradually raise North Korean economic productivity, increase food security, and provide better employment and consumer commodities for its people.

It is well-known that China's path to economic prosperity has been accomplished while preserving its one-party ruling system. But China, since the late 1970s and Deng Xiaoping, created its own brand of economic reforms that lifted hundreds of millions of ordinary Chinese people out of poverty. The official terminology of Marxist socialism has not disappeared. "[T]he overarching official rubric is still in place and thus allows the regime to subsume 'new' ideas under 'old' labels. This 'invented' continuity is a central element of the regime's strategy for staying in power ... [I]n order to survive North Korea will eventually have to follow the Chinese example and thus implement economic reforms" (Noesselt, p. 1320). The legitimacy of the Chinese one-party, state socialized capitalism could lend legitimacy for such revisionism introduced to the North Korean party elite.

The Kim regime senses its vulnerability from external forces. Certainly the United Nations' imposed sanctions make life difficult for all North Korean people. While the ruling elite prospers compared to the rest of North Korea's citizens, they understand that their deprived lifestyles compare badly to the wellbeing of their South Korean neighbors. Their lives of isolated deprivation are the price for the nuclear armaments in which the regime has invested so much and holds onto with such desperate determination. The international player with leverage to obtain denuclearization of North Korea is the People's Republic of China. Today's China wants recognition as a great power and respected participant in global affairs. North Korea's adventurism constitutes a challenge to China's positive force for world peace. Handling the North Korean challenge is a test of China's worthiness to be trusted and regarded within the international community of nations. It remains to be seen when or if China is willing to pass the test and accommodate the expectations of the major nations of the world.

Many observers in the West are skeptical of China's will to bring about denuclearization in North Korea. Cha, for example, offers this observation: "It is an illusion to believe that China will work with the United States and the ROK on denuclearizing North Korea as its top priority. China has a host of other priorities that rank higher than that of the United States and ROK, and it will follow its own path achieving them vis-à-vis the North" (Cha, p. 338). A pessimistic perspective regarding US- China relations comes from David Shambaugh:

> U.S.-China relations are not a zero-sum game, although it could devolve into one if mismanaged by both sides. The stakes are high and mutual mistrust runs deep. The relationship does have the potential to hemorrhage and deteriorate into a fuller adversarial posture if not managed intelligently. At the same time that this competitive dynamic plays out on the regional stage, Washington also needs to work effectively together with Beijing in the global arena.

> Even within Asia, both powers seek regional stability—the problem is that both see the other as contributing to instability and undermining each side's national interests. The CCP [Chinese Communist Party] also seems to see the United States as a direct threat to its existence, as is clear by its internal documents and campaigns against 'Western hostile forces.' It is difficult for Washington to deal pragmatically with a regime that views it in this negative light (quoted by Browne, *Wall Street Journal*).

There are, on the other hand, encouraging signs of movement in China. After the DPRK's 2016 nuclear test, there were weeks of heavy discussion at the United Nations about nuclear security. Interestingly, on April 1, 2016, China's Ministry of Foreign Affairs published its own National Progress Report on Nuclear Security. It did not address North Korea directly, but it set forth nine priorities for consideration at the fourth Nuclear Security Summit held in Washington. China asserted its dedication to an improved national nuclear security system as follows: "It is the fundamental responsibility of each country to maintain security of its nuclear material and facilities. China is dedicated to improving its national nuclear security system, enhancing nuclear security capabilities and boosting nuclear security culture."

It went on to state that it specifically supports the work of the International Atomic Energy Agency (IAEA), enhancing the security for highly-enriched uranium, and combating the trafficking of nuclear materials. It added this conclusion: "After the summit process concludes, China will continuously take part in a deep way in the international nuclear security process, commit to strengthen the international nuclear security system, and make contribution to strengthen global nuclear security and achieve common nuclear security for all" (Ministry of Foreign Affairs of the People's Republic of China, "National Progress Report on Nuclear Security of the People's Republic of China," April 1, 2016).

After the Summit, conducted in Washington, DC, the White House reported on the actions taken by fifty-four governing agencies (mostly individual countries) that "have strengthened nuclear security implementation … and built up the global nuclear security architecture." It summarized these actions, and specifically reported on China; to this effect, that China:

> Committed to convert the remaining Miniature Neutron Source Reactors (MNSR) at Shenzhen University from HEU to low-enriched uranium (LEU) fuel, to support the conversion of MNSR in Ghana and Nigeria as soon as possible, and – upon request of respective countries – to convert

all remaining Chinese-origin MNSR worldwide; successfully completed and officially opened the Nuclear Security Center of Excellence in Beijing on March 18, 2016; launched an Annual Nuclear Security Dialogue with the United States; passed State Security and Anti-Terrorism laws which make it clear that nuclear security is a vital aspect of national security and formulated specific tasks and measures; published a Policy Statement on Nuclear Security Culture; invited a mission by the International Physical Protection Advisory Service of the IAEA and a follow-up mission of the IAEA Integrated Regulatory Review Services for 2016; through 2015, donated U.S. $1.15 million to the IAEA Nuclear Security Fund; conducted joint exercise with Russia on preventing illicit trafficking of nuclear and other radioactive material on borders; conducted a national-level exercise on nuclear emergency response, 'SHENGDUN-2015,' with 2,900 participants and international observers; pledged commitment to INFCIRC 869 (Highlights for National Security Progress Reports, April 4, 2016).

This quite comprehensive report compares well with those regarding other American allies. It is noteworthy that Russia was not a participant in this continuing international dialogue and is not making commitments to the international community as China is. China's engagement with IAEA is a particularly welcome commitment. There is reason to believe that patient negotiations with China can eventually produce the political will in China to impose denuclearization on North Korea. Doubtless, it would necessitate a four-party (or more) treaty, in which China and the US would guarantee the continuing safety and security of both North and South Korea.

There continue to be voices of optimism about the likelihood and benefits of a peaceful reunification of the two Koreas. One of those is Koh Il Dong of the Korean Development Institute. He has made an explicit forecast about demographic change in the two Koreas in order to note that "North Korea's relatively young demographic structure can compensate for South Korea's aging population which has grown at an unprecedented level." Likewise, he comments on the complementarity of the physical and natural resources of the two Koreas.

> North Korea's abundant mineral resources represent another potential for the development of a unified Korea and economy. North Korea's advantage in its mineral wealth lies not only in its abundance but also in its diversity. Taking into account that natural resources-deficient South Korea has to import most of these minerals, endowments of those resources lying under North Korea will lay another foundation for the development of unified Korea's related industry (Koh, p. 276).

Koh acknowledges that it will take a long time to make up the income disparity for people in the North as compared to the South. He suggests a time period of twenty-five years or more. Nevertheless, in his optimism, Koh argues that "North Korea's present weak points can be another springboard for its expeditious economic development. North Korea is saddled with two critical constraints: over-militarization and strictly closed economic system. A removal of those these constraints will work as new stepping stones for a swift transformation and development of the North Korean economy" (Koh, p. 278). "Given that Korea's national division has been the greatest impediment to the economic cooperation of Northeast Asia, the unification of North and South Korea will lay a firm ground for a speedy integration of the regional economy." Koh's optimism leads him to conclude: "In Northeast Asia, any meaningful improvement of regional integration can hardly be carried out without a resolution to problems arising from North Korea. There lies the need of Korea's unification in the framework of international cooperation and integration" (Koh, p. 279).

Sue Mi Terry makes the same points of argument as Koh, but more assertively. "There can be only one happy ending to the long-running saga of the North: the emergence of a single democratic Korea. Outsiders should do all they can to promote and plan for this outcome" (Terry, 2014). She suggests three reunification scenarios for the future: China-like economic reforms in North Korea and an eventual integration with the South, thus a "soft landing"; a massive implosion of an unreformed North followed by absorption by the South; or reunification by military conflict. She calls the last improbable, the first unlikely, and the second, a hard landing, most plausible. She cautions about the costs to the ROK's economy (one estimate says $80 billion annually for ten years), but argues that "those costs would be out-weighed by the benefits of reunification." She counts up the economic positives for the US, the ROK, Japan, and China. Then she weighs in about the humanitarian benefits for the North Korean people.

> The end of the Kim regime would also have huge humanitarian benefits, freeing 25 million people from the grip of the world's last remaining Stalinist state and integrating them into a modern democracy. The majority of North Korea's 80,000 to 120,000 state prisoners could leave the government's slave-labor camps, where most have been consigned for political, rather than criminal, offenses. Average North Koreans could move from a starvation diet, both literally and intellectually, to the plentiful availability of food, information, consumer products, and all the other benefits of modern capitalism (Terry, 2014).

Terry puts the burden of rescuing North Korea from its inevitable hard landing upon the ROK and the US.

> [The] regional powers, notably South Korea and the United States, should stop propping up the Kim

dynasty in return for fleeting assurances of better behavior, as they have in the past; Kim Jong Un is no more likely to keep these promises than his father or his grandfather was ... Once the United States and South Korea develop a common vision, they should encourage Japan to join the planning ... As a final step in this process, the trilateral dialogue among the United States, South Korea, and Japan should expand to include China and possibly Russia. All these key players should be asked to bear some of the costs of reunification in return for a say in how the new Korea behaves in the region (Terry, 2014).

Terry's optimism concludes with this solution: "In fact, the best way to cope with future instability in the North and reduce the cost of reunification is for the principal powers to start cooperating now. North Korea has the worst government on the planet. Despite all the challenges a transition will entail, everyone will benefit immeasurably from the rise of a new Korea, whole and free" (Terry, 2014).

What is noteworthy about the unification arguments from Koh and Terry is that they are conceived as top-down means to put Humpty Dumpty – South and North Korea – back together again. The quest assumes a singular wholeness about the people of the peninsula. But there are secular trends that indicate growing differences and separation. Despite the efforts of the ROK's Ministry of Unification to urge and plan for putting the two Koreas together, there are contraindications becoming apparent, particularly from the younger generation of the South Korean people. Joel Brinkley reported in 2012 on the voices that he heard. " 'We don't want reunification with the North,' said Jisu Choi, a junior studying Korea's relationship with India. 'We think of them as different people in a different country. We don't really share anything with them anymore' " (Brinkley, p. 8). Brinkley perceives a dynamic of change.

South Korea is undergoing a transformative generational change – one that has strong implications for the US. The younger generation, living a comfortable life in a first-world state, cares little about the threat posed by North Korea, which has been the dominant theme of South Korean life since statehood in 1948. The North is a dilemma of their grandparents' generation that, to them, is no longer relevant ... To many members of this new inward-looking generation, the Unification Ministry is an irrelevant artifact (Brinkley, pp. 7-8).

In a 2014, the Asan Institute for Public Policy issued a public opinion report, "South Korean Attitudes toward North Korea and Reunification." It noted that in a New Year's press conference that year, President Park argued for unification by suggesting how it could produce an economic "bonanza" for the South Korean people. The report then examined surveys from 2007 to 2014, enabling an analysis of change over time. Excerpts from the executive summary are as follows:

> Data from previous recent public opinion surveys depict a South Korean public with complicated views of North Korea ... As the data make clear, perception[s] of the North Korean people are much more positive than are views of North Korea the country ... Of concern, however, is that the youngest South Koreans report the largest distance with North Koreans. This youth detachment from North Korea is perhaps the most important recurring theme in the public opinion data over the past five years ... This report takes a closer look at the opinions held by the South Korean public on North Korea and unification. These attitudes are often highly pragmatic, and seemed to indicate a public generally suffering from North Korea fatigue (Kim Jiyoon, et al., pp. 5-6).

Within the report are specific numbers by age cohort that reveal a declining sense of the importance of shared ethnicity in regard to the question about reunification. "While 75.3 percent of those 60 and older cited the ethnic component in 2007, it declined to 51.3 percent in 2014" (Kim Jiyoon, p. 21). For the other age cohorts (twenties, thirties, forties, and fifties) the percentage varied from 40.9 to 34.2. The lowest percentage was for the cohort in their forties. The report goes on to say:

> This decline in the importance of ethnic nationalism, if it continues, will undermine one of the central tenets of reunification by choice. This could very well weaken the reunification picture overall, as the Korean public has yet to fully buy in to the economic benefits that reunification could bring ... Any forecast for reunification will almost certainly mean an increased tax burden ... The good news is that a plurality (48.1%) of the South Korean people reported a willingness to pay a reunification tax ... The bad news may be that there is a wide discrepancy between age cohorts. Those in their twenties and thirties were nearly 20 percentage points less likely to support a reunification tax than their older countrymen (Kim Jiyoon, p. 22).

The conclusion ends on this pessimistic note:

> Although more than 80 percent of South Koreans dutifully answer that Korea should be reunified, less than 20 percent support immediate reunification. Most of all, it is seen as a serious economic burden ... Efforts are necessary to establish a link between the legitimacy and necessity of reunification. While its success is not guaranteed, it remains important nonetheless. In doing so, the government should take two independent tracks in dealing with North Korea. One track should deal with the North Korean regime and the other should be aimed at the North Korean people. The interest, sympathy, and ethnic bond with the North Korean people are rapidly fading. Therefore, communication and exchange on a civil level should be sustained (Kim Jiyoon, p. 23).

EPILOGUE: ACCOUNTING FOR THE POSSIBILITY OF PEACE IN THE KOREAN PENINSULA

The drama of a "failed marriage" between North and South Korea is going to be a continuing one as international relations in Northeast Asia unfold in the years ahead. But having examined the relationships between what are two distinct nations, and the stakes of the countries that have been interested in that failure, especially China, the United States, Japan and Russia, the question remains: can regional peace and relative harmony be achieved and, if so, at what cost?

I will reserve comment upon the distant future and a description of long-term outcomes. Let me first consider current realities with a family analogy. Within a nuclear family of two parents and three children, one highly disruptive child can upset relationships between each person with every other. In spite of apparent parental power to control matters, the unpredictable and upsetting actions of the disruptor interfere with normal family order at meal times, bedtimes, and for any scheduled events on the family agenda. The power of the disruptor, even if it is the smallest child, can impose enough disorder to result in a dysfunctional family with many unhappy consequences for each and every family member.

Among the countries in the neighborhood of the Korean Peninsula, North Korea is the poorest, least powerful, but naughtiest neighbor that disrupts relationships among all the others. The DPRK makes a habit of being troublesome to South Korea and the United States, as well as Japan, China, and even Russia. Its unruliness and surprising provocations can at will disrupt normalcy for the countries around it. The well-meaning neighbors sometimes try to satisfy this petulant North Korea with favors and at other times with punishment. "Go to your room without supper," as it were.

The current realities in the DPRK and the region make it plain that North Korea can continue as a disruptor for a relatively long time – I estimate at least a decade, perhaps longer. Despite North Korea's many weaknesses and deficiencies, the ruling elite has an actual nuclear arsenal and, small though it is, it has tested vehicles to deliver its weapons of mass destruction. The reality of that weaponry provides credence to Kim Jong Un's threats to begin a "merciless sacred war," as he said in his 2016 New Year's Address. Kim, it needs to be acknowledged, has made a successful accession to power. He has eliminated rivals, revamped the leadership of the Korean Workers' Party, and retired most of the military generals of his father's regime, replacing them with appointees of his own. Having dramatically called together the 7th Congress of the Korean Workers' Party, the first in thirty-six years, he has raised up the authority of the party over the military and is in a position to demobilize a portion of the uniformed army into domestic agriculture and industry. Greater productivity in food supply and consumer goods would go a long way and be a most welcome change and improvement for the impoverished lives of North Korea's common people. Such success can renew and even sustain public confidence in the *juche* doctrine, "we can go it alone." While that posture is foolish and not really true, North Korea as we now know it is not on the verge of collapse. It may be rogue, but it is not a failed state.

South Korea has maintained long-suffering patience with the provocations of its northern cousin. Whether it is encroachments by North Korean fishermen in the South's waters, insults to South Korea's presidents, efforts by the North to disrupt global positioning satellite signals for South Korean use, publicizing practice strikes on South Korean targets, or other similar disrespectful taunts, most South Korean people largely disregard them. South Korea continues to prosper with a powerful economy, a well-educated workforce, a brisk international trade, vibrant relations with other countries, including China and Japan, and effective democratic institutions. The sturdiness of the ROK's constitutional democracy was recently demonstrated by the orderly impeachment of President Park and the peaceful succession by Moon Jae In to the presidency through a fair election by the people. The younger generation in South Korea does not yearn for a unified Korea and is skeptical of what unification would cost in terms of wellbeing and quality of life. The threats from the North are largely discounted by the younger South Koreans as unrealistic.

Japan is firmly allied with South Korea and the US. Although Japan and South Korea are rivals in international trade (think of Toyota and Nissan in competition with Hyundai and Kia in the US auto market), they are solid trading partners with one another as well, with exchanges worth between $80 and $100 billion annually. Each country is the other's third largest trading partner. Japan, with a more mature economy than South Korea's, has invested more than $2 billion annually in South Korean corporations (Obe and Mochizuki, *Wall Street Journal*, December 29, 2015). These investments signal long-term commitments to trade and mutual development. Japan and South Korea have settled an enduring World War II issue regarding "comfort women." During the Japanese occupation of Korea, many Korean women were coerced by the Japanese into brothels for exploitation by the Japanese occupiers. An agreement in 2015 between South Korea and Japan called for Japan to provide $8.3 million for medical, nursing, and other services for Korean survivors. By agreeing, South Korea promised to no longer criticize Japan with regard to that issue. The US praised both nations for settling this nagging and divisive issue (Choe, *New York Times,* December 28, 2015). That resolution illustrates the capacity of these two "frenemies" to settle stubborn issues as negotiating equals. Such diplomatic prudence can and will help maintain peaceful relations in Northeast Asia.

The US is big brother to both South Korea and Japan, with wide-ranging connections to each culture and political system. The US guarantees their safety and security militarily along with other neighbors, including Taiwan and the Philippines. These are all significant trading partners and allies committed to regulated corporate enterprise (capitalism) and to democratic freedoms at home and elsewhere in the world. The US has treaty commitments to protect these countries from attack, including nuclear attack from any source, particularly the DPRK.

Although Russia extends into the Northeast Asian neighborhood, its stakes in the Korean Peninsula are much attenuated since the Cold War era. For now, at least, Russia is, as I have quoted Cha previously, "a bit player." President Vladimir Putin can encourage Kim's adventurism from afar, but Russia's major foreign policy initiatives and problems in the current world now mostly regard Syria and Ukraine. Russia's economy is teetering because the value of its oil exports have plummeted. Moreover, international trade sanctions have been imposed on Russia following its annexation of Crimea, and the Russian military meddling in Ukraine. North Korea is peripheral to its interests while South Korea is a much more substantial trading partner with Russia. However, having greatly reduced oil revenues in the last couple of years, Russia's imports from South Korea declined to $4.53 billion (US dollars) in 2015, while South Korea had imports of about $13.2 billion. (Russian Exports National Information Portal at www.rusexporter.com; data for 2015, reported for South Korea on 4/13/2016: for North Korea on 4/22/2016). In 2015, North Korean exports to

Russia were a meager $5.7 million while it received imports of $77.5 million, mostly on credit. Despite its recent trade decline, Russia receives much more benefit from trade with South Korea than with North Korea. Russia's market relationship with South Korea constitutes a good reason for maintaining favorable relationships with the ROK and for not adding capacity to the DPRK for making mischief in the region.

The People's Republic of China looms large in the present and future management of tensions caused by the DPRK and affecting the ROK, Japan, and the US. China remains as North Korea's primary patron state. It is North Korea's chief trading partner. In 2013, China bought an estimated $1.5 billion in North Korean goods, mostly coal and iron. Despite China's enduring relationship with the DPRK, after the North Korean nuclear test in January 2016, China reduced most of its imports of coal and iron, upping the effect of United Nations' sanctions against the DPRK. In June 2016, the China's Ministry of Commerce identified a detailed list of "dual use items and technologies in connection with weapons of mass destruction" that were newly banned from being exported from China to North Korea (Ministry of Commerce, announcement number 22, June 17, 2016). This is a major step in reining in the potential for North Korea to continue making aggressive military steps to intimidate its neighbors. Nevertheless, China wants to maintain a nuanced relationship with the DPRK. Near term, it does not want the DPRK to be a failed state. Such a condition would stir desperate North Koreans to become refugees, pouring into China for relief and burdening a part of China that is itself relatively impoverished and underdeveloped. "While China clearly opposes North Korea's nuclear advancement, it remains committed to North Korean stability and to obtaining leverage with Pyongyang" (Snyder and Byun, p. 107).

By contrast with its often tense relations with the DPRK, China's entirely peaceful engagement with the ROK continues to grow in both appearance and substance. In the years before her recent impeachment, South Korea's President Park and President Xi of China engaged in a series of productive face-to-face meetings, and authorized engagements by lower-level bureaucrats from each government. For example, the PRC and ROK navies conducted joint anti-piracy exercises in November 2015. It was reported that "Chinese media organizations selected Park among the top 10 people of 2015, citing her balancing role between major powers and attendance at Beijing's military parade commemorating the 70th anniversary of the end of World War II" (Snyder and Byun, p. 102). The growing substantive engagement between the China and ROK is evidenced by their recent free trade agreement. When negotiations on the agreement began, the level of trade was already $215 billion. Three years in negotiation, it was completed in 2015. The exchange value of their bilateral trade was expected to have reached $300 billion by the end of 2016 and, in a world of relative peace, it is likely to keep growing. The China-South Korea relationship is more than economic.

> The deepened China-ROK trade relationship has also emerged as a point of South Korean leverage for seeking Chinese support for Seoul's broader regional economic initiatives that ultimately link to North Korea's reform and denuclearization ... [I]mprovement in China-ROK relations lays the foundation for coordinated action between Seoul and Beijing to pressure North Korea toward denuclearization, which is also in US interests. Minimizing the gaps between Beijing and Seoul generates greater pressure and limits North Korean alternatives to denuclearization (Snyder and Byun, pp. 106-107).

Despite occasional points of contention between the United States and the People's Republic of China, these two nations share growing interdependencies. The historic opening of trade between the US and the China followed a breakthrough in bilateral relations fostered by President

Richard Nixon and Mao Zedong in China during 1972. In the decades since, the political and trade barriers increasingly fell away. By 2016, both countries have become, literally, deeply invested in one another. According to the US, goods and services trade with China totaled an estimated $659.4 billion in 2015. Exports were $161.6 billion; imports were $497.8 billion (Office of the US Trade Representative, 2015). The US goods and services trade deficit with China was $336.2 billion in 2015. China was the United States' third-largest goods export market, generating $116 billion for the United States. China was the largest supplier of goods to the US, in the amount of $482 billion. Obviously the US has a huge deficit in goods trade. Less well-known, and much less in dollars, is the exchange of services (such as travel, intellectual property, and transportation) where the US has a surplus estimated at $30 billion in 2015. Also less recognized is the fact that US dollars go to China as direct foreign investment in the stocks of corporations ($65.8 billion in 2014, the latest data available), while China's foreign direct investment in the US was $9.5 billion in 2014. Another dimension of US-China economic relations is the fact that China holds US Treasury bills, notes, and bonds in the amount of $1.2 trillion as of April 2016, a significant portion of the entire US debt of $19 trillion (Amedeo, *about.com*, 2016). The US and the PRC have huge investments in each other, thus high economic and political disincentives to relate to each other in any destructive fashion.

What may come as a surprise to many Americans is how deeply and mostly peacefully the US and China are engaged with one another. Yes, there has been dramatic video showing Chinese planes buzzing American ships and those images seem threatening. However, what is much more consequential is the working relationships at every level between the two countries. US colleges and universities are the preferred destination for Chinese students studying abroad. According to the *Wall Street Journal*, in 2015, "Chinese students accounted for nearly one-third of all 975,000 overseas pupils ... at American colleges and universities," far outnumbering foreign students from anywhere else in the world (Belkin and Jordan, *Wall Street Journal*, March 17, 2016). Presidents Obama and Xi met on a wide range of issues. After the sixth such meeting, Obama said cooperation was delivering results after candid discussions about Iran, Afghanistan, global development, global health security, humanitarian assistance, disaster response, agricultural development, and food security (Glaser and Vitello, p. 22). Not only did Obama praise President Xi, Chinese media lauded the bilateral accomplishments, saying that President Xi's visit to the US "has completely accomplished its purpose of enhancing trust in reducing suspicions" and went "better than expected" (Glaser and Vitello, p. 22).

To illustrate the degree and complexity of the China-US relations, Glaser and Vitello appended to their article seventy-three specific relationship items by date for just the last four months of 2015. Only a handful of those items identified conflicting interests, such as concerns about cyberattacks, unsafe air reconnaissance, or the Chinese build-up of the Spratly Islands. A great many more addressed shared approaches to problem solving: climate change, multilateral arms controls, illicit drug traffic, greenhouse gas emissions, business rules, cyber security, peer-to-peer military exchanges, an emergency "space hotline," and a memo of understanding about the regulation of money laundering. There is then every reason to believe that this bilateralism will enable these two world-leading nations to build confidence and trust for long-term problem solving, including a cooperative approach to North Korean aggression.

In my considered judgment, the United States and South Korea have substantially increased a broad and complementary set of consequential and peaceful relationships with the Chinese. The issues of the future, including those with the DPRK, are amenable to mutually regarding negotiations and problem solving. Meanwhile, those relationships have not diminished the essential bases for China's leverage with the DPRK. While continuing as

North Korea's closest ally, China has chosen to take part in sanctions against North Korea specifically with regard to denuclearization. China is in a position to impose its will upon the DPRK, providing incentives for the DPRK to hold on to, but not activate, its nuclear devices and missiles. If China can and does restrain the DPRK to a weapons freeze, China can provide assurances of protection to the DPRK from hostile attacks from the ROK and the US. That would establish grounds for a future treaty which would be in the interests of all four nations. A long-term accord would be welcome in the broader neighborhood, including Japan, Taiwan, and the Philippines. Such a consensus could promptly bring about a dialing down of the United Nations' sanctions, thereby permitting the DPRK to reenter the legitimate processes for international trade. Exploiting its rich raw materials for a wider market and turning its human resources into productive enterprise instead of threatening military exercises can generate capital for domestic investment and development. North Korea can even market part of its workforce into enterprises abroad. With technological assistance from China, the DPRK has the agricultural and industrial potential to multiply its productivity in the same fashion that the Chinese did a generation ago. A workforce spared the limiting burdens of military obligations can generate the tools, infrastructure, products and services needed for a more truly self-sufficient, *juche* styled society. Kim and his ruling party could, with greater legitimacy, then acclaim such accomplishments as the rewards for their faithfulness to the Workers' Party's unique ideology.

Of course, as new political figures come and go, the pace of success/failure in the four-sided relationships between and among North and South Korea and their patrons, China and the US, will undergo change. The bona fide connections and obligations that keep the four nations in tension with one another are unlikely to dissolve for an exceedingly long time. Perhaps new presidents in South Korea and the US will find novel solutions to put on the negotiating table. In particular, President Trump, acting more on pragmatic than ideological grounds, might apply his talents using "the art of making a deal" in order for all the participants to go home judging themselves to be winners. Certainly all four nations would benefit their people greatly if such a transaction could be hammered into reality. But what if that kind of winning does not take place? In a worst case scenario, the "sea of fire" that the DPRK has often threatened its neighbor with might actually be ignited. Who knows where all the flames would burn in our fraught and interdependent world if success is not achieved by negotiation and compromise?

The future prospects sketched above will not satisfy observers for whom the offences of the North Korean rulers against the human rights of its people are of paramount concern. The extent of that abuse is clearly alarming and widely confirmed. **Chapter 6** above records stories from escaped citizens, just enough to make clear the cruelty of the ruling regime. For the reader who wants a larger, up-to-date, and more detailed look at North Korea's exploitation of its people, see a report to the United Nations General Assembly by Marzuki Darusman, A/70/62, September 8, 2015. Shocking as this UN report is and previous ones are, I judge that neutralizing the DPRK's threats to impose nuclear terror upon the innocent inhabitants of Northeast Asia and beyond is an even higher humanitarian concern to the US and our allies. To illustrate, just south of the 38th parallel, the populations of Seoul and Inchon constitute over thirteen million South Koreans who literally can be held hostage by the threat of an actual nuclear attack by the North's leadership. In the language of previous threats, North Korea has the actual capacity to turn Seoul into a "sea of fire." Constraints from the international community must address this threat to world order as a matter of top priority. As already noted, the allies have focused upon defensive capabilities, with the latest wrinkle a THAAD missile defense. But defenses are not impermeable. In Seoul, a clandestinely placed nuclear weapon capable of remote triggering could cause a "sea of fire" that would make the Pearl Harbor sneak attack in 1941 and the September 11th disaster in New York in 2001 look small by comparison.

The key to long term containment of the North Korean threat is actually in the hands of the DPRK's neighbor and singular ally, the People's Republic of China. The US, South Korea, Japan, and even the United Nations cannot accomplish that constraint without unacceptable military violence. Neither do these allies nor the international community have the will to undertake such extreme measures. But China alone has the leverage to neutralize the DPRK with small but steady steps. China, less than half a century ago, was an implacable contender nation, hostile to the US and Asia's emerging democracies. But since the rise of Deng Xiaoping in 1978, China has transformed into a prospering, peaceful, competitor nation. It increasingly follows and benefits from the rules of international order. It flourishes today by means of its economic productivity, trade, and unswerving determination to gain preeminence in world affairs. Remarkably, its accumulated wealth has made it the number one creditor nation for the US. Its progress on many dimensions, including human rights, have earned it respect and deference from the other nation states. With its growing domestic security, economic development, humanistic investment in its own citizens, and wide engagement with nations around the world, it has vastly bettered the lives of its 1.4 billion people. China should and can be both model and mentor to North Korea.

The North Korean ruling regime can learn from China's successful example a new and flexible model of growth by combining vigorous private market competition with state/party-directed investment. Simply reducing the government's over-investment of scarce capital in redundant military hardware and personnel would allow it to capitalize on productive technology. In the PRC, a sagacious blending of state control wedded to some demand driven economic capitalism has lifted China, both the state and its people as consumers, to a whole new level of wellbeing. If the DPRK would follow the Chinese model for its economic development and governing strategy, it could be secured by a Chinese umbrella of military assurances and protection confirmed by a US commitment to China. Then the DPRK could securely foreswear its dependence upon a nuclear shield of its own. As a result, North Korea could ratchet down the rhetoric of its gruesome threats of merciless nuclear destruction and relate to South Korea and the US without the need for intimidation. Mutually beneficial relations across the 38th parallel could take real and significant form. Security from external threats would positively encourage North Korea with a sense of safety from a hostile external world. Moreover, investments in technology to fulfill domestic needs — including food security, goods, education, infrastructure, and human services — would alter the entire fabric of life in North Korea. These are not unrealistic, "pie in the sky, bye and bye" pipe dreams. The recoveries achieved by Germany and Japan after WWII and the growing wealth and wellbeing currently evident in what the world knows as the Socialist Republic of Vietnam, today a single nation made up of what used to be North and South Vietnam, makes the point.

The election of Moon Jae In to the South Korean presidency opens renewed hopes for a peaceful settlement on the Korean Peninsula. Moon brings a more accommodating openness to peacemaking efforts than former President Park. With regional leadership from China's President Xi, Moon can reopen economic and social relations between the two Koreas. Keep in mind that while the US has been South Korea's political ally and military protector, China is now its biggest trading partner and will continue to be for years to come. It is in China's long-term interest to use its economic leverage with both nations to lead the two Koreas into a treaty agreement. North Korea has agitated for that for some time. Its strategy to fulfill that desire has mistakenly focused on the US to make it happen. American presidents before Trump would not agree. They ignored or openly resisted one-on-one relations with the DPRK. Now, with Moon more flexible about making accommodations with North Korea and Trump pressing China to take the lead in restraining North Korea, it can be President Xi and China's turn to become the influential agent that creates change in the multilateral relationships of Asia. China controls a vast array of material resources, including oil, and commodities desperately needed by North Korea. South Korea can hugely benefit from favorable trade relationships with China and its vast population of consumers who can buy and use its products. A China-refereed treaty negotiation could provide guarantees of protection that North Korea wants, no longer necessitating its offensive nuclear weapons and allowing it to release much of its military personnel into fulfilling Kim's desire for economic development. South Korea, unthreatened by destruction from the North, could largely demobilize its standing army and be less dependent upon the US. Lessened hostilities between the North and South could open endless possibilities for incremental interaction economically, socially, culturally and, someday, even politically. The payoff for China would be the prevention, not only of nuclear devastation, but the breakdown of impoverished North Korea. China wishes never to cope with flooding millions of hungry, ill-educated, and impoverished North Korean refugees fleeing north over the Yalu River into China. Nor does it want a South Korea-United States subjugation of the North that would encroach upon its border. China prefers an enduring North Korean buffer state and the prospects at home for economic prosperity from orderly economic trade with the US and its Asian neighbors.

In a context of peace and some substantial social and economic development, the prospects for improving the human rights and wellbeing of the North Korea people can hardly worsen and may be gradually addressed in the North. In the future, can the regime evolve mechanisms of responsiveness to its people and operate by standards of justice that approximate those of the South? That is a long stretch of change and likely will require several decades of time to unfold. Certainly, however, the story of international politics is a lengthy history and, presumably, one with an enduring future. The contestation dividing the two Koreas has a seventy year history. It need not be endless. Perhaps separation with non-hostile neighborliness will be the best that can be achieved. Whether or not unification of the North with South Korea ever occurs, peaceful coexistence would make winners of both nations. But the promising way to resolve belligerence is through comprehensive intercession by China and responsive negotiations by South Korea, Japan, and the US. The US and the Northeast Asian neighbors should count the costs for a strategy to bring that about. The price and the rewards for paying it will doubtless be a vastly more affordable investment than the costs of waiting passively or interfering hostilely until risk-taking adventurism by Kim Jong Un brings on a nuclear disaster that will not be contained within the borders of the Korean Peninsula.

I fear to reflect upon the unboundedness of such an event.

BIBLIOGRAPHY FOR KOREA

Acheson, Dean. Present at the Creation: My Years in the State Department. New York: W.W. Norton & Company, 1969.

Brinkley, Joel. "No Fear or Just Smug? South Korea's Youth Dismiss the Northern Threat." World Affairs, 175, No. 4, November/December 2012, pp. 7-14.

Campbell, Angus, Philip E. Converse, Warren E. Miller and Donald E. Stokes. The American Voter. New York: John Wiley and Sons, 1960.

Cha, Victor. "A Path Less Chosun: South Korea's New Trilateral Diplomacy." Foreign Affairs, October 8, 2015. www.foreignaffairs.com/articles/china/2015-10-08/path-less-chosun

Cha, Victor. The Impossible State: North Korea, Past and Future. New York: Harper Collins Publishers, 2012.

Chapin, Emerson. "Success Story in South Korea." Foreign Affairs, April 1969. 47, No. 3. www.foreignaffairs.com/articles/asia/1969-04-01/success-story-south-korea

Chapin, Emerson. "Sato Government Faces Parliamentary Test on Japan-South Korea Treaty." New York Times, Oct.

5, 1965.

"China Bans More Exports to North Korea." The Chosun Ilbo, June 16, 2016. http://english.chosun.com/site/data/html_dir/2016/06/16/2016061600894.html

Choe Sang-hun. "Ex-Dictator's Daughter Elected President as South Korea Rejects Sharp Change." New York Times, December 19, 2012.

Choe Sang-hun. "Governing Party Retains Edge in South Korea Vote." New York Times, April 11, 2012.

Choe Sang-hun. "In Hail of Bullets and Fire, North Korea Killed Official Who Wanted Reform." New York Times, March 12, 2016.

Choe Sang-hun. "North Korean Mourners Line Streets for Kim Jong-il's Funeral." New York Times, December 28, 2011.

Choe Sang-hun. "North Korean Leader Tells Congress His Nuclear Program Brings 'Dignity.'" New York Times, May 6, 2016.

Choe Sang-hun. "South Korea is Surprised by Departure of Candidate." New York Times, November 23, 2012.

Choe Sang-hun. "With Nuclear Test, North Korea's Leader Asserts Role of Instigator." New York Times, January 8, 2016.

Chung, Joseph Sang-hoon. "North Korea's 'Seven Year Plan' (1961-70): Economic Performance and Reforms," Asian Survey, Vol. 12, No. 6 (Jun., 1972), pp. 527-545.

Croissant, Aurel. Ed. Electoral Politics in Southeast & East Asia. Singapore: Friedrich-Ebert-Stiftung, Office for Regional Co-operation in Southeast Asia, 2002 - VI, 370 S.

= 1280 KB, PDF-Files.

Cumming-Bruce, Nick. "Rights Panel Seeks Inquiry of North Korea." New York Times, March 28, 2014.

Dausman, Marzuki. "Situation of human rights in the Democratic People's Republic of Korea." United Nations General Assembly, A/70/362, September 8, 2015. http://www.securitycouncilreport.org/atf/cf/%7B65BFCF9B-6D27-4E9C-8CD3-CF6E4FF96FF9%7D/a_70_362.pdf

Demick, Barbara. Nothing to Envy: Ordinary Lives in North Korea. New York: Spiegal & Grau, 2010.

Eberstat, Nicholas. "Can the Two Koreas Be One?" Foreign Affairs, Winter 1992-93. www.foreignaffairs.com/articles/asia/1992-12-01/can-two-koreas-be-one

Facts About Korea. Korean Culture and Information Service, Ministry of Culture, Sports and Tourism, 2015 Edition. http://www.scribd.com/doc/253910595/Facts-about-Korea-2015#scribd

Ferguson,Wallace K. and Geoffrey Bruun. A Survey of European Civilization. Boston: Houghton and Mifflin, 1952, Second ed.

Fifield, Anna. "With (fake) blood and guts, U.S. Army practices for North Korean attack (Posted 2016-03-16 16:00:03): Near the setting of 'M.A.S.H.,' a field hospital was in full swing," Washington Post, March 16, 2016.

Fifield, Anna. "North Korean video apparently shows U-Va. student taking propaganda sign (Posted 2016-03-18 02:09:08): The grainy clip shows a tall man pulling down a red banner but his identity is not clear," Washington Post, March 18, 2016.

Fifield, Anna. "North Korea claims it could wipe out

Manhattan with a hydrogen bomb," Washington Post. March 13, 2016.

Fifield, Anna. "North Korea launches 'satellite,' sparks fears about long-range missile program," Washington Post, February 6, 2016.

French, Howard W. "Seoul May Loosen Its Ties to the U.S." New York Times, December 20, 2002.

Huntington, Samuel P. The Third Wave: Democratization in the Late Twentieth Century, Norman: University of Oklahoma Press, 1991.

Halberstam, David. The Coldest Winter: America and the Korean War. New York: Hyperion, 2007.

Hardin, Blaine. Escape from Camp 14: One man's Remarkable Odyssey from North Korea to Freedom in the West. New York: Penguin Books, 2013.

Hastings, Max. The Korean War. New York: Simon and Schuster, 1987.

Haggard, Stephan, Byung-kook Kim and Chung-in Moon. "The Transition to Export-led Growth in South Korea: 1954-1966." *The Journal of Asian Studies,* Vol. 50, No. 4 (Nov., 1991), pp. 850-873

Hundt, David. "A Legitimate Paradox: Neo-liberal Reform and the Return of the State in Korea." Journal of Development Studies. Vol. 41, Issue 2, (February 2005), pp.242-260.

Jackson, Van. "Putin and the Hermit Kingdom: Why Sanctions Bring Moscow and Pyongyang Closer Together." Foreign Affairs, Snapshot, February 22, 2015. www.foreignaffairs.com/articles/east-asia/2015-02-22/putin-and-hermit-kingdom

Jager, Sheila Myoshi. Brothers at War: The Unending Conflict in Korea. New York: W.W. Norton & Company, 2013.

"Kaesong Shutdowns 'Causes Losses of Over W800 Billion.'" The Chosun Ilbo. February 25, 2016. http://english.chosun.com/site/data/html_dir/2016/02/25/2016022501156.html

Kang Chol-hwan and Pierre Rigoulot, translated by Yair Reiner. The Aquariums of Pyongyang: Ten Years in the North Korean Gulag. New York Basic Books Edition, 2005. Originally published in French in 2000.

Kim Eunsun, with Sebastien Falletti, translated by David Tian. A Thousand Miles to Freedom: My Escape from North Korea. New York: St. Martin's Press, 2015.

Kim Hyung-Jin. "N. Korea vows to end diplomatic communication channel with US." Associated Press, reported in the Washington Post, July 11, 2016.

Kim Ilpyong J. and Lee Dong-Bok. "After Kim: Who and What in North Korea." World Affairs, Vol. 142, No. 4 (Spring 1980), pp. 246-267. URL: http://www.jstor.org/stable/20671834

Kim Jiyoon, Karl Friedhoff, Kang Chungku and Lee Euicheol. "South Korean Attitudes toward North Korea and Reunification." Asan Public Opinion Report. The Asan Institute for Public Policy Studies, 2015. thediplomat.com/wp.../01/thediplomat_2015-01-29_13-53-09.pdf

Kim Jong Un. New Year Day 2016 Address, accessed from http://www.kcna.kp/kcna.user.article.retrieveNewsViewInfoList.kcmsf

Kim Kihwan. "The 1997-98 Korean Financial Crisis:

Causes, Policy Response, and Lessons" Paper presentation at The High-Level Seminar on Crisis Prevention in Emerging Markets, Organized by The International Monetary Fund and The Government of Singapore. Singapore: July 10-11, 2006.

Kim, Samuel S. "North Korea's Nuclear Strategy and the Interface between International and Domestic Politics." Asian Perspective, Volume 34, Number 1, 2010, pp. 49-85.

Kim, Sunhyuk and Doh Chull Shin. Economic Crisis and Dual Transition in Korea. Seoul: Seoul National University Press, 2004.

Kissinger, Henry A. "North Korea Throws Down the Gauntlet" New York Times, June 3, 2009.

Koh, Byung Chul. "Political leadership in North Korea: Toward a conceptual understanding of Kim Il Sung's leadership behavior." Korean Studies, Volume 2, 1978, pp. 139-157.

Kotkin, Stephen. "Russia's Perpetual Geopolitics: Putin Returns to the Historical Pattern." Foreign Affairs. Comment, May/June, 2016. www.foreignaffairs.com/articles/ukraine/2016-04-18/russias-perpetual-geopolitics

Leavenworth, Stuart. "N. Korea's triumphal congress does little to win over a frustrated China." The Christian Science Monitor, May 11, 2016

Lee, Sung-Yoon, and Joshua Stanton. "North Korea's Next Dare: What Is Coming—and What to Do About It." Foreign Affairs, September 14, 2015. www.foreignaffairs.com/articles/north-korea/2015-09-14/north-koreas-next-dare

Lerner, Mitchell B.The Pueblo Incident: A Spy Ship and a Failure of American Foreign Policy. Lawrence: University Press of Kansas, 2002.

Matray, James I. "Hodge Podge: American Occupation Policy in Korea, 1945-1948." Korean Studies, 19, 1945, pp. 17-38.

Ministry of Commerce [for the People's Republic of China], Ministry of Industry and Information Technology, China Atomic Energy Authority and General Administration of Customs. "Concerning the Additional List of Dual-use Items and Technologies Banned from Export to North Korea," Announcement 22, June 17, 2016. http://english.mofcom.gov.cn/article/policyrelease/ buwei/201606/20160601348963.shtml

"Most S. Koreans Support THAAD Deployment." The Chosun Ilbo, February 16, 2016. http://english.chosun.com/site/data/html_ dir/2016/02/16/2016021601522.html

"N. Korea Endorses Donald Trump." The Chosun Ilbo, June 2, 2016. http://english.chosun.com/site/data/html_ dir/2016/06/02/2016060201615.html

"N. Korea to Liquidate S. Korean Assets." The Chosun Ilbo, March 11, 2016. http://english.chosun.com/site/data/html_ dir/2016/03/11/2016031100774.html

Noesselt, Nele. "China's contradictory role(s) in world politics: decrypting China's North Korea strategy." Third World Quarterly. August 2014, Vol. 35 Issue 7, pp. 1307-1325.

Obama, Barack. "Renewing American Leadership," Foreign Affairs, July/August 2007. www.foreignaffairs.com/ articles/2007-07-01/renewing-american-leadership

Oberdorfer, Don and Robert Carlin. The Two Koreas: A Contemporary History. New York: Basic Books, Third Edition, 2014.

Office of the US Trade Representative, 2015. https://ustr.
gov/countries-regions/china-mongolia-taiwan/peoples-re-
public-china. Accessed July 15, 2016.

Onishi, Norimitsu. "Conservative Wins Vote in South
Korea." New York Times, December 20, 2007.

Onishi, Norimitsu. "South Korea's President Sags in
Opinion Polls." New York Times, November 27, 2006.

Park Myoung-Kyu and Philo Kim. "Inter-Korean Relations
in Nuclear Politics." Asian Perspective, 34, No. 1, 2010, pp.
111-135.

Perlez, Jane, and David E. Sanger. "John Kerry Urges
China to Curb North Korea's Nuclear Pursuits." New York
Times, January 27, 2016.

Perlez, Jane and Yufan Huang. "A Hole in North Korean
Sanctions Big Enough for Coal, Oil and Used Pianos," New
York Times, March 31, 2016.

Plant, Thomas and Ben Rhode. "China, North Korea and
the Spread of Nuclear Weapons," Survival Apr/May2013,
Vol. 55 Issue 2, 61-80.

Rangel, Charles B., with Leon Wynter, ...And I Haven't
Had a Bad Day Since: From the Streets of Harlem to the
Halls of Congress. New York: St. Martin's Press, 2007.

Romberg, Alan D. "New Stirrings in Asia," World Politics,
1985 America & the World, Vol. 64 Issue 3, pp. 515-
538. www.foreignaffairs.com/articles/asia/1986-02-01/
new-stirrings-asia

Savada, Andrea Matles and William R. Shaw, eds. South
Korea, a country study. Washington: Federal Research
Division, Library of Congress, 4th ed., 1992.

Schilling, John. "A New Submarine-Launched Ballistic Missile for North Korea" 38 North, April 25, 2016. http://38north.org/2016/04/jschilling042516/

Schilling, John. "Three (or Four) Strikes for the Musudan?" 38 North, June 1, 2016. http://38north.org/2016/06/jschilling060115/

Sheehan, Neil. A Fiery Peace in a Cold War. New York: Random House, 2009.

Shin, Doh Chull, and Rollin F. Tusalem, "Partisanship and Democatization," Journal of Asian Studies, 7 (2007), pp. 323-343.

Shin, Doh Chull, and Jason Wells, "Is Democracy the Only Game in Town?" Journal of Democracy, 16, Number 2, April 2005, pp. 88-101.

Shin, Doh C., "The Evolution of Popular Support for Democracy during Kim Young Sam's Government," in Larry Diamond and Doh Chull Shin, eds., Institutional Reform and Consolidation in Korea. Stanford: Hoover Institution Press, pp. 233-256.

Stokes, Henry Scott. "The Rise of Chun Doo Hwan." New York Times. Sept. 22, 1980. http://search.proquest.com/docview/121099299?accountid=14554

Terry, Sue Mi. "A Korea Whole and Free." Foreign Affairs, Jul/Aug2014, Vol. 93, Issue 4, pp. 153-162.

Trumbull, Robert. "Korean Election Augurs Stability: President's Victory Shows Widening of Power Base Assembly Election in June Few Major Infractions." New York Times. May 5, 1967: 14.

US Department of State. "Report on Human Rights Abuses and Censorship in North Korea." July 6, 2016, accessed at http://www.state.gov/j/drl/rls/259366.htm.

Wada Haruki, translated by Frank Baldwin. The Korean War: An International History. Lanham, MD: Rowman & Littlefield, 2013.

For More News About Jack Van Der Slik Signup For Our Newsletter:

http://wbp.bz/newsletter

Word-of-mouth is critical to an author's long-term success. If you appreciated this book please leave a review on the Amazon sales page:

http://wbp.bz/tkca

ANOTHER GREAT READ FROM WILDBLUE PRESS!

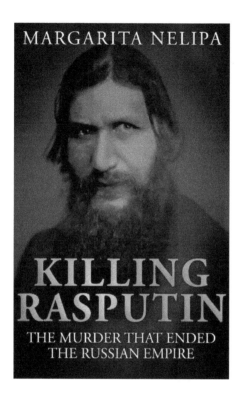

"*A fresh and compelling look at one of history's most controversial, and perhaps misunderstood, characters. You can almost hear the whispering conspiracies and intrigues in the court of Nicholas and Alexandra. ... A dramatic history with a touch of true crime.*"—**Steve Jackson,** New York Times bestselling author of **NO STONE UNTURNED**

http://wbp.bz/killingrasputin

 See even more at:
http://wbp.bz/tc

More True Crime You'll Love From WildBlue Press

BOGEYMAN: He Was Every Parent's Nightmare by Steve Jackson *"A master class in true crime reporting. He writes with both muscle and heart."* (Gregg Olsen, New York Time bestselling author). A national true crime bestseller about the efforts of tenacious Texas lawmen to solve the cold case murders of three little girls and hold their killer accountable for his horrific crimes by New York Times bestselling author Steve Jackson. *"Absorbing and haunting!"* (Ron Franscell, national bestselling author and journalist)

wbp.bz/bogeyman

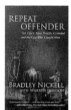

REPEAT OFFENDER by Bradley Nickell *"Best True Crime Book of 2015"* (Suspense Magazine) A "Sin City" cop recounts his efforts to catch one of the most prolific criminals to ever walk the neon-lit streets of Las Vegas. *"If you like mayhem, madness, and suspense, Repeat Offender is the book to read."* (Aphrodite Jones, New York Times bestselling author)

wbp.bz/ro

DADDY'S LITTLE SECRET by Denise Wallace *"An engrossing true story."* (John Ferak, bestselling author of Failure Of Justice, Body Of Proof, and Dixie's Last Stand) Daddy's Little Secret is the poignant true crime story about a daughter who, upon her father's murder, learns of his secret double-life. She had looked the other way about other hidden facets of his life - deadly secrets that could help his killer escape the death penalty, should she come forward.

wbp.bz/dls

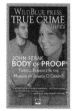

BODY OF PROOF by John Ferak *"A superbly crafted tale of murder and mystery."* – (Jim Hollock, author of award-winning BORN TO LOSE) When Jessica O'Grady, a tall, starry-eyed Omaha co-ed, disappeared in May 2006, leaving behind only a blood-stained mattress, her "Mr. Right," Christopher Edwards, became the suspect. Forensic evidence gathered by CSI stalwart Dave Kofoed, a man driven to solve high-profile murders, was used to convict Edwards. But was the evidence tainted? A true crime thriller written by bestselling author and award-winning journalist John Ferak.

wbp.bz/bop

CPSIA information can be obtained
at www.ICGtesting.com
Printed in the USA
LVHW03s1728170718
584088LV00017B/1303/P